## The Insider's Guide to Buying a Car

Bill Robinson bought his first car, an Austin 1100, in 1975. It cost £300 and lasted just six months before expiring on the way to the coast. His current vehicle, a Volvo estate was bought at auction in 1997 for £130 and has so far served him for 18,000 trouble-free miles. In between, he owned, used, bought and sold many hundreds of cars from Reliant Robins to Range Rovers, primarily whilst working as a salesman with new and used car franchises and as a self-employed 'bombsite' trader. Latterly, Bill Robinson has been employed by the police and in that capacity has encountered many vehicles that have been stolen, 'ringed', or dangerous and often shoddily rebuilt accident write-offs. This book was written in response to requests from friends for him to accompany them when buying cars.

# The Insider's Guide to Buying a Car

BILL ROBINSON

ROBERT HALE · LONDON

© Bill Robinson 1999
First published in Great Britain 1999

ISBN 0 7090 6393 8

Robert Hale Limited
Clerkenwell House
Clerkenwell Green
London EC1R 0HT

The right of Bill Robinson to be identified as
author of this work has been asserted by him
in accordance with the Copyright, Designs and
Patents Act 1988.

2 4 6 8 10 9 7 5 3 1

Typeset in North Wales by
Derek Doyle & Associates, Mold, Flintshire.
Printed in Great Britain by
St Edmundsbury Press Limited, Bury St Edmunds
and bound by
WBC Book Manufacturers Limited, Bridgend.

# Contents

*List of Illustrations*   7
*Introduction*   9

| | | |
|---|---|---|
| 1 | The Car Trade – An Overview | 13 |
| 2 | New or Used? | 27 |
| 3 | New-Car Prices | 39 |
| 4 | Used-Car Prices | 45 |
| 5 | Part-Exchange Deals | 53 |
| 6 | Initial Approach and How to Assess Vehicles | 61 |
| 7 | Stolen Vehicles and Accident Write-offs | 73 |
| 8 | The Salesmen | 85 |
| 9 | Special Offers and Finance Deals | 95 |
| 10 | Warranties | 107 |
| 11 | Doing the Deal | 113 |
| 12 | Auctions – How They Operate | 129 |
| 13 | Selling Your Car Privately | 145 |

*Glossary of Terms and Abbreviations*   153

# Illustrations

*Between pages 80 and 81*

1. A sure 'ringer' with warped VIN plate and poorly fitted rivets
2. An obvious mistake made by a thief when ringing a vehicle
3. A 'clocked' odometer showing misaligned numbers
4. Paint overspray on window rubbers and glass indicating a cheap respray
5. Uneven tyre wear which could be the result of a badly repaired accident write-off
6. A Calibra, stolen and stripped for parts, which will be repaired and back on sale in no time

# Introduction

Every year millions of people from all walks of life buy motor vehicles from car dealers. Annual sales of new cars alone are over two million. The vehicles taken in part exchange against them will generate another two million used-car sales, and these in turn will lead to even more sales, as trade-ins are taken against them. Typically, the buyers will return in two or three years' time to trade in their current vehicle for a newer one, and go on doing so for most of their adult life. This pattern is reflected throughout the developed world.

Yet, ask these buyers how the price of their vehicle was calculated, and the vast majority would confess to having no idea. The motor trade is shrouded in a mystery that is fiercely protected and propagated by its members; there is a legacy of secrecy reminiscent of a Masonic lodge. Virtually no one outside the trade knows how it works. Car dealers both large and small advertise a bewildering array of special offers, guaranteed part-exchange prices, finance deals and free gifts, all of them designed to mask the real price of their deals and thus prevent the customer – you – from comparing like with like. In addition, the trade is riddled with criminals and shady operators selling stolen cars, rebuilt write-offs and tarted-up bangers. Thousands of people are ripped off every year. And you could be one of them, unless you know what to look out for!

It is often said that, after buying a house, buying a car is the largest single expenditure of most people's lifetimes. But most people buy more cars in their lifetime than they do houses, so they may actually end up spending more on the wheels underneath them than on the roof over their heads. It is also said that house-buying generates a level of stress that is surpassed only by bereavement and divorce. But when you negotiate a house purchase, your path is smoothed by professional experts – surveyors, solicitors, estate agents and mortgage advisers – who are all on your side. When you buy a car, it is just you versus the salesman: eyeball to eyeball with a professional hit man! It is hardly surprising, therefore, that even hardened businessmen balk at car-buying. Most people (and here we are talking about the vast majority of car-buyers) never know whether they have got a good deal.

There is a tremendous psychological pressure on a buyer entering a car showroom – particularly on those buying a used car. People have become conditioned to fearing the worst. There are so many uncertainties: Can the salesman be trusted?; Is the car going to be reliable? You do not even know what price you are paying: How can one dealer offer £500 more for your part exchange than another?; What is the catch with 0% finance? Because of these fears, customers are easily manipulated by skilful salesmen. They need to be reassured, and they need to get the deal done and get the hell out of there, while the salesman feels relaxed and in control – he is on home territory, and he is an expert at selling cars!

There are ways around this seemingly unfair disadvantage, though. For one thing, a salesman is used to people agreeing with what he says (after all, he is the expert) but – providing

*Introduction*

you do your homework (as explained later in the book) before you enter negotiations – you will be able to control the flow of the negotiations. If you really want them to, many salesmen will come to your home or office to discuss any deal that you may be considering; this further strengthens your position, because it is you, and not the salesman, who is on home territory.

Make no mistake, buying cars can be a veritable minefield. Apart from a house, it may be the only thing you ever buy that you will bargain for. But, when you buy a house, an estate agent acts as a neutral buffer in negotiations, which preserves a modicum of civility. Purchasing a car, though, calls for one-to-one dealings. These are contrary to British custom, a fact that the trade exploits. Customers are by and large vulnerable to the professional negotiators – the salesmen. Any conversation between customer and salesman is seen as a conflict: one wanting to buy the exact make, model and specification of his choice at the minimum cost; the other trying to extract the most money, whilst subtly trying to steer the deal towards the old stock model that has been eating into his commission for months. This need not be the case though. A salesman, if handled correctly, can work for you rather than against you and can be a powerful ally.

This book explains how prices and part-exchanges are calculated; what profit margins there are, and how you can eat into them; which special offers are really worth having; how to avoid the hidden pitfalls, and when and where to get the best deals. It shows how to deal with salesmen on your terms. A chapter is devoted to the assessment of cars, from reading advertisements to test drives; this will enable you not only to avoid fruitless journeys to look at unsuitable vehicles, but also to identify back-street traders masquerading as private sellers, and so avoid buying someone else's problems. A further chapter explains how to spot the ringers, clocked cars, former taxis and accident rebuilds. Buying at auction can yield exceptional bargains – and present huge risks. Two chapters are devoted to covering this increasingly popular method of buying. From main dealers to bombsite pitches, private sales and damaged repairables, all the avenues are covered with hints, to help the buyer avoid both buying a dog or paying too much for a mint example. In understanding the machinations of the motor trade, whether it be a main dealer in Mayfair or a bombsite in Bolton, you will see the true price of any car offered and be able, confidently, to strike the best deal for yourself.

# 1 The Car Trade – An Overview

Dodgy men in sheepskin coats, resprayed bangers and old caravans: that is how the trade is epitomised, the cliché continually represented by television programmes such as *Minder* and *EastEnders*. In reality, the car trade is a multi-million pound business that uses cutting-edge technology and the latest marketing methods. Vehicle manufacturers rely greatly on the advertising industry to ensure that their products become embedded in our minds and leap to the forefront when triggered by words, music or images used in advertisements. You cannot listen to M People's hit *Search for the hero* without picturing a Peugeot racing through burning sugar cane; mention the words 'Velly tough as old boot' and everyone expects a Golf to come crashing down from the ceiling, even though the VW advert has not been shown for over ten years. Such is the hidden power of advertising. The annual advertising budget for the motor trade is over eight hundred million pounds, three-quarters of which is funded by vehicle manufacturers. Even allowing for the commercial vehicle side, that is almost £300 per new car sold. Indeed Vauxhall are reputed to pay their ad men more than they spend on the metal that goes into their vehicles. The new car industry is thoroughly researched and planned, with nothing left to chance. Every new model endures hours of rigorous testing and is subjected to customer clinics, where it is assessed by ordinary people, before it enters production.

Cars are part of our lives – a big part of some people's – and thousands of millions of pounds are spent every year on cars, parts and accessories. They become part of our language, our dreams and aspirations. People will readily get hopelessly into debt to buy something that means so much to them and so little to anyone else. One's car has become the accepted status symbol, a reflection of oneself. Whether you like it or not people judge you as a person on what you drive – and, of course, you make similar assumptions about them. Car magazines fuel such dreams, allowing us mere mortals to appreciate what it is like to drive rare and expensive machinery. We become experts without actually seeing the car in the metal. Like football supporters, we will align ourselves behind certain marques and scoff at the supposed faults of their rivals. Ask people what they would buy first if they won the lottery, and I guarantee that over 75% will nominate a particular car. Rarely a month goes by without some magazine running an article pigeon-holing car-owners into categories such as sporty, dull, considerate, etc., based on what they drive.

Psychology plays a big part in the car trade, and the industry thrives on making dreams come true. You are what you drive: that is why we are easy prey to skilled salesmen. Manufacturers constantly update models, adding new and sometimes unnecessary features to distinguish the later edition from earlier ones. At least one of these 'improvements' will be visible externally – different trim, a badge or redesigned headlights – just to make sure that the change is obvious to everyone. This creates consumer demand. People feel the need to keep up with fashion (just look at how, over the last few years, the shape of cars has gone from round to square and back again). Buyers will even find themselves justifying the need for sixteen valves and round headlights. They will wonder how they ever managed with only two valves per cylinder, and, as for those square headlights ... well, they never looked right. The pride of their life (two years ago) will seem wholly inadequate when compared with the new object of their desire. All those niggling little faults will assume great importance and suddenly be impossible to live with. You, not the salesman, will convince yourself to change your car and buy a particular model, solely on the basis of advertising or sales literature.

New car franchises, although independently owned, are strictly controlled by manufacturers, who determine each dealership's territory, stock levels and the rate of discounts. A dealership will be allowed a certain number of new cars in any one financial year. If it fails to hit its sales target, then its allowed stock may be reduced the following year. Find a dealership that is struggling to meet its target, and you will be in a very strong negotiating position. Conversely, if a dealer outsells his target, his stockholding may subsequently be increased. However, if a particular dealer is extremely successful and far outstrips his anticipated annual sales, then he may find it difficult to obtain the extra vehicles, especially if neighbouring branches are also exceeding supply. Franchises in this situation will be reluctant to do deals that do not involve a part exchange unless the gross profit in the sale makes it worthwhile.

Companies like Ford, Vauxhall, Rover, etc., employ area managers to ensure that the manufacturer's interests are best served. This is ever more important, now that modern retailers often represent many different marques. Selling cars is big business, and there is no room for sentiment. Whereas traditionally companies remained loyal to the same manufacturer, they now think nothing of changing to a more profitable brand. For their part, manufacturers are constantly striving to increase their market share, both through model launches and improvements and by obtaining prime selling sites. Particularly if their local dealership is underperforming, or lacks the capability to expand, makers often canvass successful companies selling rival marques, to try and convert them to their own brand. In the past certain dealerships have played musical chairs to an extent that has brought their customer credibility into question – people naturally expect that the supplier of their new car will hang around long enough to carry out its 1,000-mile service. In some cases companies have closed down overnight and quickly reopened with a different logo over the door. Believe me, loyalty – to brand or customer – is a rare commodity in the motor trade.

A motor manufacturer's corporate identity is important to create a link with national advertising. Its dealers are expected to comply with the manufacturer's campaigns and even to lay out their premises according to a master plan that is consistent throughout the country. This ensures that the customers attracted by media advertising identify with the premises immediately. Even the advertising is centrally controlled. If you travel to a different part of the country and buy a local newspaper the adverts will look familiar. Every Ford dealer uses identical corporate templates in its advertising, as do dealers for Rover, Vauxhall, Toyota, etc.

This marriage between manufacturer and dealer is not totally harmonious. Car makers would love you to test-drive their models, and they regularly advertise test-drive offers. If you take up their invitation, however, it is the dealer who must organise your demonstration drive, at his expense. He has not got the time or inclination to allow people not committed to buying to drive around in his cars. He would much rather you took his competitor's car for a spin, then came back to deal.

In any given area or territory there are likely to be several competing franchises selling the same make. Usually these will be a large main dealer, who may have many branches nationwide, and several smaller garages, possibly family-owned. The small dealers rely on the goodwill of their larger competitor, who will hold many more cars in stock than they do. Taking just one model as an example – whether it be a Ford Galaxy or Toyota Corolla – the availability of different engines, number of doors, etc., may create fifteen or sixteen variants of that model, each of which could come in one of at least eight colours. That gives well over 120 permutations – without even considering manufacturer's optional extras, like sun roofs, air-conditioning, alloy wheels or alternative upholstery colours. A small dealership cannot hope to stock all these variations and therefore will hold a selection of the most popular choices. However, Murphy's Law dictates that the customer always orders what is not in stock, so the small dealer must go cap in hand to his big brother in order to swap or borrow the required car to close the sale. This brings business ethics into play. There are only so many customers per area. If Mr Smith, who is shopping around for his Galaxy diesel in gold with black upholstery and alloy wheels, visits the main dealer first, then the small garage may have difficulty in getting hold of that vehicle if they subsequently offer him a better deal. The main dealer's Sales Manager will be aware that one of his sales team has had a recent customer for exactly this specification, and that his counterpart from down the road is now trying to secure such a car. He will guess that Mr Smith is dickering with his small competitor and may block the swap. He may then even immediately canvass Mr Smith, knowing that he is ready to deal and that they already have his vehicle in stock. By the time the frustrated salesman at the smaller garage has phoned around the country to secure another vehicle, Mr Smith may be back up the road signing on the dotted line.

There is an exception to this arrangement: the showrooms operated by the Korean company Daewoo. This manufacturer has tried to revolutionise the way in which we buy new cars. It owns all its new-car outlets, and so has a greater control over distribution. One major difference in its policy is that all salesmen receive a set wage, and no commission payments are made. In theory this should mean that customers are not pressurised into any deal. The idea of selling new cars in this way, through supermarkets and even mail order is an old one and apparently straightforward.

It would seem that the customer cannot lose. However, although new cars are what economists would call a perfect commodity – you can buy an identical item from any dealer – used cars are all individually unique – and this is where the major stumbling block arises: what do you do with your old car? It is apparent that the British car owner cannot grasp the basic principle that any used vehicle is only worth its trade price. It does not matter whether you sell it at auction, drive into a dealer's premises and ask him to buy it, or trade it in against another car – it will be valued the same, at the trade price. If you can sell your car privately, then you will probably get more than a dealer would offer and make an effective saving on the whole deal, but this is uncertain and means hassle. It is much simpler to drive into a garage in the old car and drive out in the new one, and, if you are blind to the potential saving, then it doesn't hurt.

Increased access to Europe and the current strength of the pound has led some punters to hop over the water and save several thousand pounds on modest family cars. In this instance they *have* to dispose of the old car, as even Arthur Daley's French cousin can't sell right-hand-drive Escorts in Paris. What is particularly interesting about these foreign purchases is that very few customers seem actually to obtain the best deal abroad that they could. Most are so blinded by the savings in lower retail prices, taxes and other duties that they forget about the dealer's profit margin, which will be roughly the same as that of his British counterpart; if they shopped around and made the foreign salesmen pitch for their business, then there is no reason why they could not make a further saving of around £800 on a typical family saloon, and much more on luxury motors.

New-car franchises must by necessity take part exchanges, and therefore sell used cars too (in actual fact it would be difficult for a dealership to survive on new-car profits alone). The sale of used cars supplements the profit margins. So does the supply of accessories, parts and servicing. For every new car sold, the service department gains a customer, and when the car is serviced it obviously requires parts – oil, filters, spark plugs and the like. These are all invoiced at full retail price, so the parts department flourishes too. Many people also purchase customised accessories, and around 40% of their retail price goes into the dealer's pocket. Many car parts are 'dealer only': that is, they are only available through the manufacturers. For popular cars, common wearing components, such as brake shoes and wheel bearings, are often made by specialist spares manufacturers and sold cheaply in the ubiquitous car spares shops; the volume of sales warrants competition in production. But spare parts for less popular cars, parts that rarely require replacing and major components are often available only from the vehicle manufacturer, and often at a much higher price than most people expect to pay. This monopoly creates welcome profits for dealers.

The trade-in vehicle may require mechanical or body work repairs before being sold, so more internal business is generated. If it breaks down during the warranty period then most new owners will contact the sellers in the first instance; the warranty company pays for the repairs, and the service department carries them out. You may have realised by now that the car-selling aspect is only the catalyst for a dealership's profits.

Used-car dealers range from the purveyors of fine motor vehicles from grand showrooms with marbled floors and exotic pot plants, right down to fenced-in bomb sites with a leaky caravan for an office. They can be placed into broad bands or categories according to their stock vehicles' age and condition. New-car dealers usually have a range of used vehicles up to three or four years old. The older cars tend to be pristine examples, with low mileage, one owner and a complete service history. In the main these vehicles will be part exchanges taken in against new cars. Some dealers, however, buy job lots of hire cars or manufacturer's representatives' vehicles to supplement their stock. This is particularly true of franchises selling cars extensively used by company reps. Because the bulk of their sales are to firms, they do not get the part exchanges in the normal way, because most fleet managers dispose of old stock through auctions. Specialised used-car outlets favour vehicles from around two to six years old. This bracket includes those ex-company cars with a full service history and a zillion miles on the clock. This is the type of dealership that advertises all those confusing deals – 'Cash Back', 'Guaranteed £1,000 Part Exchange' and '0% Finance', to name but a few.

Within these two bands there are similarities in the dealers' operations as far as the customer is concerned. On entering the forecourt area or showroom you are likely to be greeted by a salesman. This is the first tier of the sale structure. He will interrogate you, in the nicest possible way, to establish:

a) Your commitment to doing a deal today.
b) Who or what he is up against: i.e. another dealer, or the different makes and models you are considering.
c) How you intend to pay the balance.
d) How much you expect for your car or what discount are you looking for.

If you intimate that you are still undecided and are testing the market he is unlikely to offer a test drive or spend much time with you. He will, however, try to obtain your name and phone number for future reference. But if you let him believe that you are in a position to sign up immediately, then he will move heaven and earth to keep you. Test drive? No problem. Coffee? As much as you can drink.

Once you have entered into negotiations you will be influenced by the Sales Manager. Not that you will actually meet this chap – indeed, some people still believe that Sales Managers, like leprechauns, only exist in fairy-tales. Your attentive salesman disappears into the darkest corner of the building to confer with this guru of prices. He subsequently returns armed with a deal, or rather a range of deals (you will not be offered their bottom line first). If you finally accept his generous offer and need a loan for the balance, you will then be introduced to the Finance Manager – who is basically a senior salesman who can add up (but, apparently, is incapable of uttering the words: 'Total Credit Price'). He will only quote the monthly or (if he thinks you are really poor) weekly repayments. When you have signed on the dotted line, in triplicate, he loses all interest in you and disappears whence he came, leaving the original salesman to sort out the finer points of delivery.

The third band of used-car dealer encompasses the bombsite and back-street garage stocked with cars from around five to ten years old or more. Here the advertising may emphasise a cheap screen price or low-deposit finance in order to attract customers onto the forecourt. Many are now specialising in offering finance to customers with court judgements against them or those regarded as bad credit risks. All negotiations will be conducted with the salesman/manager/finance expert and chief mechanic in his caravan. Here there will be none of the niceties of the larger companies: a spade is called a spade, and a car in rough condition is called a dog, especially if you are expecting to part-exchange it. Hire-purchase may be arranged, but the credit charges will make your eyes water. Guarantees are typically seven days for minor faults, like the windscreen wipers falling off, or, if a warranty is offered, three months for major mechanical breakdowns (something like the crankshaft breaking). In that case the insurers may agree to pay 50% of the total cost, excluding labour, up to a maximum of £100.

Peripheral to all this are the car auctions, where Joe Bloggs can rub shoulders with the traders and buy a car at their prices. Auction houses have done much to dispel the trade-only stigma and made themselves more open to the private buyer; some of the popular weekend sales even provide picnic areas. They may also run periodic special sales of prestige cars, company cars, goods vehicles, accident write-offs or even stolen and recovered vehicles.

Buying a car at auction can provide the best bargain of your life, or the worst. Even experienced traders get caught out sometimes, but that is mainly when they take risks. If you know how to minimise the risks, then you should be OK. Many people are under the misapprehension that auctions deal only in the rubbish that reputable car dealers will not touch. This could not be further from the truth. Often you will find pristine examples of prestige marques coming under the hammer, some of them only a few months old. Many large firms, including hire car companies and those operating representatives' and management vehicles, dispose of surplus stock through auctions. It has proved to be a quick, reliable and honest method of selling. Apart from these company-owned vehicles, there are many good-quality cars coming in from the trade itself. If they are overstocked with a particular model, dealers may send a part-exchange vehicle, so as to get a quick return of its value. Auctions have an undeserved reputation based on a long-gone, seedy past. They are now a major retailing force and are trying hard to eradicate the public's misconceptions.

For the purpose of this book, I have also incorporated some aspects of dealing with the private seller. It is often difficult to distinguish between genuine private sellers and small-time traders who fail to place the obligatory (T), signifying trade, alongside their adverts. Buying privately can be more risky than dealing with a trader. For one thing you are not covered by the Sale of Goods Act; anything bought privately is 'sold as seen'.

In the marketing sense the car trade is unique in three major ways. Firstly, with new cars the major manufacturers do not allow direct like-for-like comparisons. If you are shopping for shoes, electrical goods or even washing-powder you can find the competing brands side by side in any retailer. Cars are different, though. You will never find new Fords and Vauxhalls in the same showroom, which makes comparisons difficult. (It also ensures that the customers who have been attracted into the showroom by the expensive corporate advertising of one company do not find anything better to spend their money on).

Secondly, a car is likely to be one of few expensive items for which you will bargain. This alone causes a great deal of stress, even in hard-headed businessmen. Haggling does not come easily to most people's nature, and the time span between car purchases, typically two to three years, does nothing to make it second nature.

Finally a car is probably the only non-business purchase that you will make knowing that you are ultimately going to sell it. Furniture, electrical goods and other consumables are usually kept until they expire and then thrown out. At the end of your ownership a car is likely to be used in partial payment for its replacement, so resale values should form part of the buying equation.

The car trade clings doggedly to these unique anomalies, because it is in its interest to do so. If you are to strike the best deal, it is important to understand how the various factions operate, how prices are fixed, what margins sellers work on, and how dealers try to cloud the issue with special deals, masking expensive small print. It is also a good idea to spend some time making preparatory calculations before visiting the showroom or sales pitch. After all, you will be playing

## The Car Trade – An Overview

away from home against a more experienced opponent. 'Forewarned is forearmed' is a good motto for the car-buyer.

## 2  New or Used?

### How New is New?

What is a new car? If you believe the advertising press it could be anything up to two years old. (Many used-car companies offer ex-hire cars and other recent fleet vehicles as new – they are not new; they are used!) But in actual fact, the definition of a new car is one that has not previously been registered. In practice, this can mean that a car manufactured in 1997 could be first registered to a buyer in late 1999, and it would still be considered new. This happens all the time. There are fields, old aerodromes and car-parks containing hundreds of thousands of new cars of virtually every make – all unregistered and waiting to be transported to dealers.

The range of new cars offered is enormous. Six or seven variations on a model is not uncommon; multiply that by up to 12 colour schemes, incorporate trim options, and you may have over 400 listed variants of just one model range, before allowing for manufacturer-fitted options, such as sun roofs, etc. Dealers cannot be expected to stock every single variation, so the manufacturers' agents hold a huge pool of vehicles, including a representation of the less popular lines. Sometimes these vehicles spend months if not years waiting for a buyer. Dealers order vehicles from the concessionaire, typically on a monthly basis. The buyer, who is a senior member of the management team, tries to predict what will sell in the following few weeks and, after allowing for current stock, orders accordingly. He will rarely take a risk and request something that has only limited appeal (unless the manufacturer puts pressure on him to take slow-movers or offers an incentive), so the bulk of his order will be bread-and-butter models in popular colours. When manufacturers change or update their models it leaves a pool of old stock, mostly the less attractive models and colours. These are sold by means of discounting to make their prices more attractive than those of the newer models. (Sometimes, however, a dealer or concessionaire may be stuck with something that just *will* not sell: a lime-green Lada, for example. These cars linger on in showrooms or gently rust out in the compound until someone with a bobble hat and anorak can be persuaded that he really can afford a brand new car, and that his Reliant Robin will make full deposit.)

One way of checking when the car was manufactured is to look at the vehicle identification number plate under the bonnet. The actual VIN is made up of a series of codes indicating the model, place and time of manufacture and colour. Frequently there will be two numbers amongst the letters – XYZ96ABC, for example. In this case it identifies a 1996 model. For cars that do not follow this format, you can still check by noting the VIN and telephoning the manufacturer or concessionaire. It may take a while, and you may have to be persistent, but ultimately they will oblige.

When a new model is brought out all the old ones that have not been invoiced are rounded up and shipped out at a healthy reduction to dealers who specialise in this type of business. They buy them by the thousand and advertise heavily. People naturally want the latest edition, and the price of the newer model has been raised accordingly. This creates a substantial difference between the newer model and the older one. (It also has a knock-on effect on the old model's price when you eventually trade it in – but they do not tell you that.) Sometimes brand-new, unregistered cars drop in price so dramatically that they are actually cheaper than recently registered demonstrators run by dealers. In these instances the company will either hang onto their demonstrators until the stock runs out or, more usually, reduce the prices accordingly.

Quite often you find that a newly introduced model sells alongside its predecessor for quite a few months. In these instances the old model is priced temptingly lower than the update or replacement. Before choosing the 'bargain', though, consider that in two or three years' time, when you are due to trade in again, used-car buyers will naturally want the more recent model, as opposed to the older one, and this will cause the resale price of the older model to be considerably lower than that of a newer model of the same age, mileage and condition. It would not be unusual for there to be a 25% difference – something to consider now rather than later.

## Working Out the Cost Implications

Before deciding whether to buy a new or used car it would be sensible for you to work out whether you can afford it. This might sound obvious but, believe me, most people do not bother, and they end up paying more than they can afford or having a car that they cannot afford to run. Only you know your real budget. But if you do not sit down and work it out properly, then you will be prey to the finance man and the temptation to go for a dearer car. When considering a car purchase, the monthly payments, or how much cash you require out of the bank, should be the last part of the equation.

Before that is calculated you need to know the running costs of your choices. Running costs encompass things like insurance, fuel, servicing, road tax and wearing items, like tyres and exhausts. Do you know how much the insurance will be on the new car? You might be in for a shock. If buying a brand-new car or nearly new car, can you afford the dealer's service charges? Some main dealers will bill you £40 and upwards an hour even for routine servicing. If you do not have it dealer serviced, then the warranty will lapse.

If it is a used car, what abut reliability? What are parts prices like? A wheel bearing for a Vauxhall may cost a third of that of a Volvo or VW. You can phone around local garages and ask the price of servicing or repairing common faults – fitting brake shoes or replacing exhausts, for example – for the various cars of your choice. In your local library will be consumer magazines and general car magazines incorporating car tests. These often indicate service intervals and reliability, based on reader surveys, and before contemplating any particular car it may be worth consulting such journals. When looking at published surveys, only consider those from reputable sources, such as motoring organisations or consumer associations. There are a lot of so-called surveys that are unreliable because too small a database has been used, or because manufacturers have vested interests in the results.

Fuel costs can also be calculated using the manufacturers' figures found in car magazines. Diesel engines return better fuel-consumption figures, but when considering whether to buy a petrol or diesel model you must also take servicing and repair bills into account. Theoretically diesel engines are simpler and ultimately more reliable than petrol counterparts:

## New or Used?

they do not have any complicated ignition systems or engine management units which can prove expensive to repair. In the 1980s, when Peugeot was making giant strides in quiet, smooth diesel options for family cars, it appeared that before long all cars would be oil-burners. That was when the price of a gallon of diesel offered a significant saving compared with petrol. Nowadays the price per litre in this country is the same, or in some cases slightly higher for diesel. And, whilst diesels still do substantially more miles for a given quantity of fuel, the saving may be eroded by higher servicing and repair costs: when a diesel does break down it is often serious. The service charges vary from model to model and garage to garage, of course, but for new-car buyers, who are tied to main-dealer servicing for the first two or three years, this can prove expensive. As for reliability, you may fall between two stools. If you are buying new the reliability benefit will only become apparent if you keep the car for significantly longer than the manufacturer's warranty period. If you are purchasing a used diesel, then always be aware that the major attraction of these cars is their economy for high-mileage users – the car will have been to the moon and back. Low-mileage diesels are as rare as rocking-horse manure. Balance fuel economy against servicing bills when calculating running costs.

Depreciation is the biggest single expense of running a car. Yet most people do not even consider it. Some cars depreciate 25% as soon as you register them, others may only drop a couple of percent in the first year; the difference could be thousands of pounds. If you had purchased a new car in August 1995 with a budget of £10,000 then you might have considered the Ford Escort, Vauxhall Astra, Honda Civic, Rover 200, Toyota Corolla, VW Golf, Nissan Almera, Peugeot 306 and the Fiat Punto, all of which would have retailed within a couple of hundred pounds of that figure. Two years on, one of these cars has a trade valuation of about £7,800, whilst another is valued at around £5,600. That is over £20 per week difference! This depreciation directly affects your budget when you come to trade in the car. It can make the difference between affording the car of your choice and making do with a lower specification.

Traditionally, there are considerably fewer new car registrations in June and December. In June, customers tend to wait for August's licence-plate prefix change before taking delivery; in December, many wait until the change of calendar year in January alters the official year of registration. This causes a cash-flow problem for dealers, who receive payment only after the new car has been delivered. To compensate, manufacturers try to stimulate sales of new vehicles with special offers, including reductions of retail prices. However, a two- or three-year-old car registered just before the prefix change and bearing the earlier letter for that year would, when part-exchanged, be valued at around 5% less than a car registered later in the same year. On a £5,000 used car the difference will be around £250; this may well be less than the discount offered to register the new car before August. The December deal is not so beneficial. A used car registered in December of any year will retail at a price substantially less than one put on the road a few days later in January of the following calendar year. The more expensive the vehicle, and the newer it is when resold, the more you will lose. It is too early as yet to predict exactly what effect the proposed dual prefix changes will have on used-car prices. What is certain is that a car bearing the later letter will be worth more than an otherwise similar car which has the earlier prefix. Check the used-car guides before making up your mind when to buy a

*New or Used?*

new car. Balance depreciation against special offers.

Unpopularity can manifest itself in part exchanges too. There are certain cars that dealers welcome onto their forecourt, and there are those that they will not have on their pitch at any price. This is not snobbery but hard-headed business sense. At one time the trade had a philosophy that any car will sell at the right price, but nowadays the emphasis is on increasing profitability year on year. A dealer only has so much selling space and must ensure that every square inch is used to its maximum benefit. Slow sellers will not be stocked unless the profit margin is large enough to make it worth the dealer's while.

Why are some cars heavily advertised with special deals, such as low-rate finance or high part exchange allowances? Look around the adverts and you will see that it is the same makes that are repeatedly featured in these deals. Why aren't the other marques discounted? Because they sell on their own merits without inducements. If you buy a car that is advertised at a discount on the pages of every car magazine in the country then do not expect it to be in demand two or three years later when you trade it in. The mere fact that it has been discounted will already have had an effect on the guide price; when you get round to selling it, the market will be flooded with similar cars bought at the same time as yours. It is generally the case that if new-car dealers are reluctant to reduce their prices, then that model will hold its value in the second-hand market. You cannot have it both ways. A £600 discount on a new car may be offset by an extra £2,000 depreciation when you come to sell it.

So, when considering your budget allow for depreciation. Examine the used-car price guides before deciding on a particular make or model, and look at the cost when new of a two- or three-year-old car compared with its current trade price. You will find that some makes and models depreciate far quicker than others. What seems like a bargain at this end may not be so three years on. Only when you are sure that you can afford to run the car should you work out your buying budget.

Most new-car franchises will invariably stock more of their own marques on the used-car pitch, simply because of repeat buying. They will, however, attempt to provide a balanced selection of vehicles, and if they find that they are overstocked in one particular model then they will not bid too highly on similar cars offered in part exchange. They are unlikely to give up much of their gross profit when there is no means of clawing it back on a subsequent used-car sale. The dealer may, however, offer a part-exchanged used car to other companies (subject to him doing the deal), a process that is called underwriting. Some franchises, though, specialise in quality pre-owned vehicles of their own marque, and a motorist part-exchanging a pristine, low-mileage car such as a VW or Honda will invariably be offered more at dealers that sell new cars of that make. Other new-car dealers are less choosy and prefer to offer a catholic choice. These are the ones that advertise in double-page spreads listing a confusing but attractive multitude of special offers.

Most people, including myself, borrow money for their cars, changing them as the current loan expires and taking out more credit. If you have the cash in the bank then I envy you. Should you be in this fortunate position, do not fall for the salesman's old ploy of leaving the money where it is and taking out finance. He has a valid argument in one respect but, if you decide to take out a loan, you would be better served borrowing from your bank.

## New or Used?

Whatever your means of financing the purchase, consider whether you are going to stretch yourself to afford the super-dooper model, or buy the cheaper one comfortably and fit some extras. The difference between a 'L' model and a 'GL' may be over a thousand pounds. Look at what you get for the extra money; sometimes the dearer model has little more than fancy seats and a better stereo. Consider whether you really need the extra specification. This is particularly relevant with engine size. Would you be better taking the cheaper option and having some extras of your choice fitted?

Manufacturers load their models with features – they need to differentiate between last year's specification and the new one in order to stimulate sales. It has become an obsession among vehicle manufacturers to add or change something every year. Their brochures enthuse over insignificant and often irrelevant revisions, such as changing the clock from digital to analogue, and over the years various makers have introduced revolutionary new gadgets only to discontinue them on the succeeding model. A lot of these features are of no benefit to you. Take cruise control: if most of your annual mileage is in an urban environment, you would probably never use it. Metallic paint is another cosmetic expense, as are alloy wheels and body kits. Do not fall into the trap of simply accepting that all features are benefits. Check the manufacturers' and dealers' catalogues to see what is available, and only value those that are important to you personally. Air-conditioning, for example, will be welcomed both by those who commute through city centres and asthma sufferers. Similarly, automatic transmission is a feature that would benefit commuters. Also remember that any dealer-fitted extras are eligible for a discount, but only if you ask.

Many people find themselves in the grey area between

buying new or nearly new. I have never bought a brand-new car and probably never will, though I have sold hundreds. I quickly realised that the honour of being the first name in the log book may cost up to a quarter of the drive-away price. Whatever the rate of depreciation, as soon as you put your name to the new car then it is worth the same as the salesman's demonstrator. Say the demonstrator, or 'management car' as they are commonly known, is £1,500 less than the invoice price of your new car, which you intend to keep for two years. You are paying just less than £15 per week for the privilege of having your name as the first in the log book: that is £1,500 over and above the normal used-car depreciation. If your car has been driven in from another dealer as part of a swap, then it may even have more miles on the clock than a newly registered dealer's car (assuming, of course, that the odometer had not been disconnected for the journey). Believe me it happens – the next time you are passed on the motorway by a brand-new car on trade plates, remember that it's on its way to be delivered to an unsuspecting buyer, with 16 miles on the clock!

The reason that most new-car buyers give to justify their extravagance is that in buying a new car they can ensure that it is 'run in' properly. For those of you who are under 50, 'running in' was something that you did with Morris Minors and Ford Anglias – new cars proudly sported a sticker 'Running In – Please Pass' – but once the year-letter system was introduced new-car buyers did not need to advertise their acquisition in that way. Years ago, cars were not manufactured to the same tolerances that modern machinery is (mechanics can no longer make a sideline out of salvaging the swarf out of oil changes). Modern cars do not need the same kind of initial baby-sitting, and any engine wear caused by heavy early use

*New or Used?*

will not manifest itself until after 50,000 miles at least – by which time your car will probably have been part-exchanged against a new one, and it is no longer your problem. In any case, the car may have already been hammered down the motorway by a delivery driver, so negating all your love and care. Nearly-new used cars can present the better deal in the long run. In reality the difference in value between one- and two-owner cars, especially where a dealer's or manufacturer's name is included is minimal.

So, new or used? Only you can decide. Make up your own mind before going to the showrooms. Work out all the facts and figures, leave nothing to chance. When you enter negotiations do not be swayed from your chosen path without first going away and studying the new option. Impulses cost money.

### Quick Tips

Check the year of manufacture on the VIN.
Look out, or ask for, old stock bargains (but, beware of those that will depreciate quickly or be difficult to part-exchange in a couple of years' time).
Work out your personal buying and running budget before buying.
Consider 'demonstrators' or low-mileage used cars rather than new ones.

# 3 New-Car Prices

Here we are only discussing brand-new, unregistered cars – yours would be the first and only name in the log-book. Some dealers advertise 'new' cars that have already been registered either to them or to another company. These cars may have been registered to claim sales bonuses during a campaign, and they may have sat on the pitch for over six months without turning a wheel. They may even have all the plastic seat covers intact, but if they have a number plate fitted, a tax disc in the window (though sometimes these are cashed in straight after registration) or a log book with someone's name in it, then they are used.

Before setting out to buy a new car it is important to understand how selling prices are arrived at. They are made up of the following constituents:

The manufacturer's list price
Government Car Tax
Delivery charges
VAT
Road Fund Licence

The manufacturer's list price (MLP) incorporates the dealer's profit margin, typically 15% to 20% depending on manufacturer, model, etc. It is from this profit margin that discounts are given. Should the car dealer be a little coy or reticent about exactly how much profit there is in a car, simply phone up the manufacturers or concessionaires – they will oblige. You will find their telephone number in the brochures. Contrary to popular belief, the dealers' profit margins in new cars are roughly consistent throughout Europe; the constituents that differ are the manufacturers' profit margins, car tax and VAT. If you are contemplating buying from one of the foreign companies advertising massive discounts on new-car purchases, remember that their prices do not include any discount on the MLP (they rather hope that the savings to be gained by dodging duty will cloud your mind to this fact). If you have the resources and ability to negotiate or barter with foreign dealers then there are substantial further savings to be made.

Government Car Tax is a non-negotiable fee payable on all new cars. It is not payable on commercial vehicles, unless they have been adapted to include rear seats and rear windows.

Delivery charges reflect the costs that the dealer incurs in having the car transported, stored and valeted, fixing number plates and carrying out a pre-delivery safety inspection and service (PDI). It can vary from one dealer to the next, so be sure to compare this when shopping around. This figure may include any fuel included with the 'drive-away' deal (the difference between a full tank and a gallon could be over thirty quid – remember to ask).

VAT is payable on the manufacturer's list price (less any discount), Car Tax and dealer's delivery charge. (It strikes me as odd that we should pay VAT on Car Tax, but there we are!)

It is important to remember that any discount offered on a new car means less VAT is payable. Therefore, if a dealer offers to reduce the *selling* price of a new car by £400, it will actually only cost him around £340, assuming a VAT rate of 17.5%. If he offers to reduce the *manufacturer's list price* by £400, then the ultimate saving to you would be £470. This can be exploited in part-exchange deals, more of which later.

Any road fund licence offered with a car will be charged at the going rate.

Many dealers are not invoiced by the manufacturer for the vehicles supplied to them until around one to two months after delivery. They are then charged either in full or in a series of instalments. Obviously it is in the dealer's interest to sell cars quickly, for any that linger attract stocking costs, such as interest. Ideally, a dealer will hope to sell his stock before payment is due, thus helping cash flow and reducing borrowing. Salesmen, too, will be keen to turn stock over quickly, as their bonus or commission is eroded by old-stock penalties.

If a manufacturer raises prices, only the vehicles that have not yet been invoiced are charged at the higher rate. This leaves a pool of vehicles available at the previous (lower) price. If you are not too fussy about colour or trim, there are bargains to be had by phoning around different dealers and getting them to search out the old stock and lower-price vehicles on their computerised stock list. Larger new-car franchises often have access to vehicles all over the country and may be able to locate a suitable bargain.

From time to time throughout the year, notably at times of historically low sales – February and June for example – special offers may be advertised on new cars. These special offers usually amount to the manufacturer giving bonuses to dealers to promote sales. The more they sell, the bigger their bonus on any corresponding sales. Competition among the competing franchises is fierce at these times, as it is fatal to be left behind. If one dealer achieves his bonus quickly, then he will be able to undercut the price of his local rivals selling the same make of vehicle, thus creating an even bigger gulf as the bonus structure is climbed. (You can usually tell when these offers are on, as both the manufacturer and the dealers will be advertising heavily.) To preserve fairness, the bonus schemes are calculated on dealers' previous business, creating a handicap-type system under which small franchises have lower targets than large dealers. The bonuses are often paid on cars that are registered, rather than actually sold. Therefore companies will often register 'demonstrators' in their own name in order to climb the bonus scale. These one-previous-owner cars with a couple of hundred miles on the clock are often sold at a healthy discount compared with new (i.e. unregistered) vehicles after the promotion has finished.

Some companies produce abbreviated price lists lumping the manufacturer's list price, car tax and VAT together. (If this is the case, ask the salesman for a breakdown of the constituent elements, or phone, fax or write to the manufacturer or concessionaire for a full list.) As a percentage of the full retail selling price (i.e. the 'on-the-road price') the dealer's gross profit is less than 14%. Out of this margin must come your discount, as well as contributions towards the dealer's costs and overheads: wages, stock charges, rates, etc. When you consider that confectionery carries profits of 30 – 40%, and greetings cards half as much again, no wonder the poor car-dealer feels maligned when he is portrayed as a money-grabbing twister.

From time to time some manufacturers bring out special-edition models. These may have an enhanced specification and be priced accordingly higher, but they may also be of a lower specification than the base model – especially if that is generally well equipped in its class – and be priced considerably lower. The purpose of the lower-priced specials is to bring customers into the showroom: the manufacturers advertise the cars in the national media, emphasising their price, but once the customers are into the showroom the sales team will try to sell them the base model, or a higher one, by demonstrating their added features. Quite often in these cases the dealer will suffer a reduced profit margin on the specials, and therefore encourages the sales team to sell the more expensive and profitable models.

Of course you may not get a discount. If the dealer has a healthy demand, and/or supply problems, then he may not wish to fritter away his margins. You would be very lucky to get any concession on the price of a well-specified limited-edition model unless it failed to grab the public's interest. Companies such as Ford market their special editions and new models months before the launch date, and by the time the cars hit the showrooms many orders have been taken. The power of advertising is such that customers will buy blind, i.e. without actually seeing the car. (Remember the problems Mercedes encountered with their new A class: thousands had been ordered and paid for when the 'moose test' threw a spanner in the works – people had ordered the car without having the slightest inclination of what it would actually be like to drive.) All the early sales of a new model or limited edition will be at full retail price; no discount will be offered. When new models are announced manufacturers cannot deliver enough cars to meet the combined demands of customer orders, dealer demonstrators and nominal stock levels, so if you really must be the first in your neighbourhood to have a latest edition then do not expect to get a discount.

Some dealers retail cars that are always in short supply. This is particularly true of prestige marques, such as Mercedes – though others, such as Honda and Audi dealers, are often in the fortunate position of facing a demand that exceeds supply. When a salesman is reluctant to relinquish his profit margin to you he is probably not trying to do you down. He would not dare – he can only survive by being competitive, and if he charged more than his neighbouring franchises then he would go out of business quickly. If you believe that a salesman is not giving you the best deal, then shop around.

### Quick Tips

Calculate the gross profit, using dealers' price lists.
If you are not particular about colour or trim, ask the dealer to find you a bargain on his stock list.
Look out for sales campaigns indicating bigger discounts – but remember to allow for previous-year or -letter depreciation.
Optional extras are eligible for discounts too.

# 4  Used-Car Prices

Used-car prices are calculated differently from those of new cars. The first – and fundamental – point to remember is that all used-car prices are based on the trade price. In an ideal world the trade price should be consistent from one dealer to another, but, human nature and business methods being what they are, this is rarely the case. All the same, the trade price of any used car taken in for part exchange should not vary by a great deal. More often than not, when a dealer 'underwrites' a part exchange with other traders, they will bid within £25 of one another.

Most people have heard of the *Glass's Guide*, the car trade's bible. But what is seldom if ever understood is that the figures it gives are (as the name suggests) a *guide* – not an inflexible price to be applied to all cars. The *Guide* catalogues almost all cars and goods vehicles sold in this country by make, model and year, listing the suggested retail price (often called 'top book') and the trade price (or 'bottom book'). Where a model has been superseded or given a major face lift, the *Guide* will list two prices for the period when both types are on sale together. Obviously in nearly all cases the later model will be valued higher than its predecessor, although the classic exception was the MGB that was superseded in 1976 due to safety regulations in the USA – the 1975 chrome-bumper models always fetched far more than the later rubber-bumper cars. Modern-day marketing people rarely make the same mistakes.

Bottom book represents the suggested trade price of a vehicle in average condition and with an average mileage: one that would need nothing other than a quick valet before it was put on the sales pitch. If such a car existed and was sold to another trader, then that is the price it should bring. But, if you think about it, the *Guide* prices cannot be religiously and uniformly employed. If you took two identical, brand-new cars out of the showroom, sold them on the same day and then assessed them two years later their prices would differ. One might have been used by a chain-smoking commercial traveller who took his dog to the coast every weekend; it would have covered 60,000 miles and have the scars to prove it. The other could have been owned by Mr Fastidious, who immediately fitted seat covers and plastic mats; it would be in mint condition with less than 10,000 miles on the clock. They are the same car make and model of car, of the same year and with the same letter, but would you expect them to be priced the same? Of course not. That is why the trade only uses the *Guide* figures as a starting-point for interpretation.

Colour plays a large part in the trade price, and ultimately in the retail price, of used cars. There are some colours that just look right on a particular model, irrespective of what is in fashion. Traders will always ask what colour a car is before making a bid. Common colours such as white, mid-blue and pillar-box red will not attract any premium, whereas some of the more subtle shades, and especially metallics, will always be highly regarded. Fashions change, and anything that is purchased to fill a current trend or to create an impression will be out of date by the time trade-in time comes around; in severe cases – where a colour is so garish it causes comment – it might prove difficult to sell privately. Customising also reduces the vehicle's appeal to the majority of buyers.

The company that produces the *Guide* checks the prices of vehicles, both trade and retail, nationally. The suggested figures are an average, based on their translation of the whole market, but they do not allow for local demands and idiosyncrasies. A four-wheel-drive Subaru estate car, for example, would sell for a higher price in a rural, farming-based community than in a city centre. An Alfa Romeo, on the other hand, would fetch more in an urban market. (Some traders make a living by buying locally unfashionable cars cheaply and reselling them in a more suitable location.) *Glass's Guide* also does not allow for other factors, such as exceptionally high or low mileage, poor mechanics or bodywork, fitted extras, or even colours and trim. These are left to the discretion of the potential trade buyer to interpret into a value. (The listings of popular representatives' vehicles does include a business mileage valuation based on a high annual mileage).

In Great Britain we have a system of registration-mark prefixes and suffixes by which to date vehicles. The letter changes on 1 August every year, prompting a rush of new car sales (for years the motor trade has been lobbying the Government to abandon the scheme, arguing that it creates an artificial environment). In respect of used-car pricing it creates a hidden second tier of car values. Most traders assume that the *Guide* figure relates to a car that is 'on the letter', i.e. has been registered between 1 August and 31 December, and so bears the later of the two letters that can be applied to a year. Cars that were registered before August will be marked down around 5%. It must be remembered, too, that many of the new cars sold during the March – June period may have been discounted as part of a sales drive.

Much more interesting are those cars that were registered in December. Take a car that went on the road on 31 December against a 1 January registration. Even if the cars are identical in every respect, the January car will be worth hundreds, if not thousands, more at a subsequent trade-in. Again, like the August example above, the December car will undoubtedly have been reduced in price as part of a sales promotion, but the resulting discount on the brand-new price will not nearly cover the difference in the trade-in price between this and an identical January car. It is all too easy to opt for the front-end discount and forget about the rear-end penalty, but, if you do this, you do yourself no favours in the long run.

The government have finally bowed to pressure from the motor trade and announced that the registration system will change in 1999 to ensure a more even flow of new-car sales. Its proposals entail changing the prefix letter twice a year, in March and September, instead of once in August. Obviously it is too early to predict exactly how this will affect used-vehicle valuations but, it is safe to assume that the major influence will remain the year of registration. (If I were to hazard a guess, then I would suggest that a March car would be worth around 1 – 2% more than a January- or February-registered vehicle, and that a car put on the road from September onwards would fetch around 3 – 4% more than that. But, this is only a considered opinion, and it will take a few years for the trade to establish these values). What is relatively certain is that there will be a virtual absence of new-car buyers in February, and from October to the end of the year. Manufacturers and dealers will undoubtedly run tempting special deals in those periods.

Top book is the recommended selling or retail price of a

## Used-Car Prices

used vehicle. The difference between it and bottom book (the buying price) varies according to the price level (higher price, larger margin), age (older cars need more work to make them saleable) and model (some models are known to deteriorate quicker than others). Once again, there are no allowances for extras or colours that may or may not be in fashion, etc.

Every month when *Glass's Guide* is published, Sales Managers review their prices. Generally speaking, almost all their used vehicles will have depreciated in price, according to the *Guide*. On cheaper, older models the fall could be as little as £10, but nearly new cars, particularly those which do not hold their values, will have been written down substantially more. Not all cars depreciate, though – some classics actually go up in value from month to month, but these are the exception rather than the rule.

Companies who subscribe to *Glass's Guide* do so on the understanding that they should not allow the book to be passed on to anyone else. This adds to the secrecy element of the *Guide*, and it is almost impossible for you to see, let alone obtain, a copy. In due course the books are passed on to other traders who are deemed not to be eligible to subscribe to the *Guide*, or are too mean to buy it, and those carried by small car-dealers and auction traders will be one or two months out of date. (If you were to look closely you would find that the cover, bearing the subscriber's details, will be missing, to avoid any comeback on the person who passed that copy on.) However, there are similar guides to trade and retail prices available from newsagents. There are several to choose from, and they will suffice for your purposes.

A dealer will have a current stock list, and each used car will have four prices written beside it. The first is the trade price – what it was valued at when brought into stock. Then there is the revised trade price – what the car is now valued at, given the monthly depreciation. The third item is the buying-in price (for a car bought from the trade this and the trade price will – or should – be the same, but for a car taken in part exchange the buying-in price could be substantially higher – the difference being the over-allowance offered on the deal which brought it into stock). The buying-in price is particularly important for VAT purposes, because on used-car sales VAT is payable by the dealer on the difference between the buying-in price and the invoiced selling price. Finally there will be the retail price, or screen price as it is commonly known.

In August and January, when the traditional rush to buy new cars is in full swing, the flood of part exchanges entering the system causes the book prices to be written down considerably; this is simply the law of supply and demand. However, the Sales Manager does not rush out and reduce the screen price of all of his cars accordingly; the loss is generally absorbed by internal accounts. Sales Managers will review each car individually and make reductions to the screen price only when absolutely necessary, since it is a matter of honour in the trade that a Sales Manager can properly assess part-exchange vehicles and those offered to him by traders. Reducing the price of a car goes against the grain for him, because it could be seen as a sign that he has lost his skill or judgement. Every car that sticks on the forecourt is a reminder that he may have made a mistake – not that he would admit as much; he will prefer to believe that it is just bad luck, or that his customers would not know a good car if they saw one.

When a car is depreciated by reducing the trade price, the amount lost is invariably carried by the sales team in reduced commission. Most large vehicle-retailers pay salesmen a pittance in fixed wages, supplemented by bonuses on sales. When the monthly sales commissions are calculated, a reduction is made in relation to stock losses accumulated in that month for all the used vehicles on the forecourt. If a car has lingered on the forecourt for some months, the revised trade price will be considerably less than the initial trade price; when the vehicle is finally sold the commission is calculated on the lower, revised price. This system ensures that old stock is pushed to the forefront of the sales team's minds.

The final screen price displayed can vary by hundreds, if not thousands, of pounds from that suggested in the *Guide*, depending on the dealer's methods of calculating part-exchange allowances. Some display low screen prices to attract customers onto the forecourt. Others inflate the price so as to be able to offer massive trade-in allowances or other special offers.

The difference between top and bottom book prices could be called the dealer's gross profit. Out of this he will have to pay VAT (on the difference between the price he paid for the car and the selling price), all costs incurred while the vehicle was up for sale and any discount offered, whether it be in that form or in 'over-allowance' on a part exchange. Over-allowance is the term used to describe the discount offered in a part-exchange deal. Basically, it is the difference between the true trade price of your vehicle – i.e. what it would be expected to fetch at auction or when sold to a trader – and what they have actually offered for it. As a rough rule of thumb it should equate to the discount that would have been allowed by the seller if no part exchange had been offered. So, if the dealer values your car at £3,000 trade and allows you £500 of his £800 profit margin, he will give you £3,500 for the car, and the over-allowance will be £500.

## Quick Tips

Remember, the foundation of any deal is the trade price of any used car. This should be the same from one dealer to the next and reflect what the car would fetch at a trade auction.

Every used car is unique. You will never find two identical in age, mileage, condition, colour, trim, etc.

Dealers will try and move old stock first – if the salesman seems keen to push any particular car then it may be for the benefit of his commission.

# 5 Part-Exchange Deals

Assume you have a three-year-old car with 72,000 miles on the clock. It has a dent in the wing but is otherwise in reasonably good condition, and you intend to trade it in for a new model.

When the salesman assesses your car he will note the following points: make, model, year and prefix letter, colour, mileage, expiry date of MOT if applicable, expiry date of vehicle excise licence. He will then examine the vehicle and make notes on the condition of bodywork, tyres, interior trim and upholstery, and he may take a test drive to enable him to check the mechanical side of things. This summary will then be taken to his Sales Manager who will assess it as follows. He will write the *Glass's Guide* bottom book price at the top of a sheet of paper. Because your car has twice the average mileage he will make an appropriate deduction from this – say £500. The cost of bodywork repairs will also be deducted – another £150. If he has spotted the nearly bald spare tyre you can expect another £40 off. Further reductions will be made for any local or personal reasons: black cars may not sell very well in that locality for example, or he may be wary that the MOT is due and dock you £200 to allow for any unforeseen repairs. Cars registered before 1 August in any given year will carry the earlier prefix for that year and will typically be marked down around 5%. Conversely, if the car appeals in any way he may add something for this. Sun roofs are popular, for example, and could be worth up to £50. If you have kept the service record up to date and had it stamped at every service, the Sales Manager may credit you with £100 or more, partly offsetting the high-mileage penalty.

Once these additions and subtractions have been made, the result is a figure that represents what your car is worth to the trade, and this trade price is the foundation of your proposed deal. It will not change no matter what car you intend to buy; the part-exchange price you are offered against different cars will vary according to the profit margins on those cars and any devious special offers that may have inflated this profit margin, but the trade price will remain constant. This principle is fundamental to any deal that you are contemplating and cannot be emphasised enough. Put simply, your car is worth roughly the same whether you trade it in at your local garage, drive to the other end of the country and deal, sell it to a trader or put it through a trade auction. There should be no monetary disadvantage if you opt for an arrangement that does not involve a part exchange (such as buying from an auction or purchasing from abroad), and so dispose of your old car through a trade buyer. If you sell it at auction, though, providing your car is half decent, you may gain a few hundred if a private buyer takes a shine to it and outbids the traders, as often happens.

How much of the dealer's profit margin in the car that you wish to buy will be relinquished depends to a great extent on your own car and your ability to deal. As discussed in Chapter 1, each dealer sells cars of a certain age and type. If the car you want to part-exchange would not fit in with his current stock it will be sold out to the trade, which diminishes his profit washout – his cumulative profit on the deal. Providing your car is one that he would retail himself, then the dealer may take a reduced profit on the car he is selling you in order to make money on the one he is buying from you in part exchange. (This is particularly true where the car you are looking to buy has been in stock for a while. Changing stock generates people who come to look, which in turn generates sales. There is nothing more depressing for a car trader than seeing the same tired old cars on his forecourt every morning.)

Obviously, though, some models will sell better than others. Even if you genuinely believe that your Reliant Rialto is the equal of any Japanese model, public opinion is against you, so the trade will mark it down; privately, the dealer may even agree with you, but if his customers avoid such makes, then he will not stock them. It is amazing what some people regard as 'collector's cars' and expect a premium price for them. As far as the general car trade is concerned, there is no such thing as a collector's car – cars are for selling, not hoarding. (Some people might collect cars, but they do not usually shop on dealers' forecourts.) It is, as they say, horses for courses. If his pitch is full of family cars the dealer would have difficulty selling an antique. However, if you think he is not taking your Austin Allegro Vanden Plas seriously, then sell it privately (alternatively, write directly to Lord Montagu, or contact the Allegro owners club and ask if either of their members are interested in buying it).

If the company is overstocked (either in general, or with cars similar to yours), of if your trade-in is one that he would not sell himself, the dealer may phone around local car-traders and offer it to them. This is known as underwriting. The dealer will offer your car to other traders, subject to his doing the deal with you, and whatever price is offered will form his trade valuation. Or he may calculate the trade price himself and take a gamble by shipping your part-exchange out to auction. However, if you own a particularly desirable model, he may choose to look upon it in a more favourable light and take less profit on the new car he sells you in the hope of making a bigger profit on the sale of the trade-in he is buying from you.

The Sales Manager assesses the deal not just on the profit margin in the car that you want to buy but also on the potential profit in your part exchange. He then works out an upper and lower figure between which to deal. He may give the salesman a range of say £500 to go at, and this £500 is the most the salesman can offer you above the trade price already calculated (you will not of course be offered the full amount in the first instance, as the dealer's commission and reputation depend on high profits). The price offered will be made up of the trade price of your vehicle, plus up to £500. How much of the possible extra £500 you receive will depend on your negotiating skills. If you are really good at bartering, or the company needs the deal (so as to clear old stock or hit a sales target) the salesman may go scurrying back to his manager for authorisation to allow you more.

If you really begin to squeeze them for a better deal and they sense that you are ready to sign up immediately if you get it, they may offer slightly more than they would like and offset the extra cost with some creative accounting. If the car you are buying is a new one, but your part exchange is not a car they would sell via their own used-car operation, but would be sold on at auction or to another dealer, then they may bring it into stock at the trade price and discount the manufacturer's list price of the new car. At current VAT rates this reduces the amount of VAT payable by £14.89 for every £100 knocked off the list price.* So if the dealer allows you the bare trade price for your part exchange and discounts the MLP of the new car, he effectively gains 14.89% of extra discount – though how much or how little *you* benefit from this tax avoidance depends on your negotiating skills. A lot of companies do not explain this practice to you. The first that you know about it is when you see the invoice, and by then they have absorbed the extra cash.

On used cars, VAT is payable on the difference between the buying-in price and the selling price. There is usually some scope to reduce the VAT payable on used cars, but it is not as cut and dried as on new models. If the car that you are looking at has been bought in at an auction or from the trade, then there will be room to rejig the figures. But if it has been taken in part exchange against a newer car, then the chances are that the reduction will be negligible. All the same, if you don't ask, you don't get.

A higher part-exchange price can often be negotiated if you accept the dealer's in-house finance. Sometimes, though, the 'document fee', or high APR, reduces or negates the extra offered.

The all-important figure to remember (you can discard the rest) is the 'price to change': the net cost to you of changing your car. It is no good berating a dealer because the garage up the road has offered you £800 more for your car if their screen

---

* A £100 price that includes VAT at 17.5% is made up of a basic price of £85.11, plus £14.89 of VAT. Therefore if a dealer reduces the selling price by £500.00, he only has to reduce his MLP by £425.55 (£425.55 plus 17.5% VAT = £500.02). However, if he reduces the MLP by £500.00, then the selling price is reduced by a further £87.50, because you do not have to pay VAT on that £500.00 (£500.00 plus 17.5% VAT = £587.50). Not only do you save money, you also get a free maths lesson!

price is also £800 more than that of the car you are now looking at – the 'price to change' is the same. Whether you are paying by cash or a finance deal, compare only the bottom line: the amount you make the cheque out for, or the total of the monthly payments. That is the only true comparison.

All well and good, you may say, but how do I know what the trade price of my car will be? One way is to contact the car-traders who advertise in your local newspaper; the advertisements will read something like 'Cars bought for cash. Any make up to 10 years old'. Give them a ring and ask for a price for your car. The trader will offer you, at best, the basic trade price for your vehicle, and he will initially try to get it for a lower figure. Most people are horrified at this paltry valuation, so the canny trader will initially ask you on the phone what price you want. He will not waste his time viewing cars whose owners want top book or more (you would be surprised what figures some people value their own cars at). If you tell the dealer that you want the best price and refuse to be drawn into quoting a figure, then he will come and view the car. Such dealers buy most of their cars from sellers who are down on their luck and need the cash quickly. (Some of their acquisitions also come from people who have balked at a dealer's part-exchange price, done a no-part-exchange deal and then tried to sell the old car privately for more, but without success – as their new car's delivery date draws ever nearer, they become desperate for the cash.) Dealers will naturally only offer up to trade price. They can buy cars at trade price through other dealers and auctions, so they will show not even the merest hint of generosity, despite any sob stories. If one of these dealers does buy your car, then he will pay cash and take it away immediately – before you change your mind.

Another way to establish the trade price of your car is for

you to calculate it yourself. To do this, you must assess your car in the same way that a dealer would. But you *must* do it honestly, or the exercise is pointless. Look at cars similar to yours on local dealers' forecourts and work out an average retail price. How does this compete with the used-car guide price for your car? Any variance may be down to local preferences. Whatever the local difference is, add or subtract it from the magazine's trade price. Then, using this figure as a base, assess your own car. For every 10,000 miles above or below average, deduct or add 5% (average is around 12,000 for the first three years and 8,000 per year thereafter). Reduce the figure to compensate for any paintwork that needs doing or any obvious mechanical problems that will need sorting. Remember, too, that worn tyres, cracks in windscreens, torn seats, all have a detrimental effect on the trade price.

Once you have honestly assessed the car, work out the final figure. That should be the true trade price of your car, there or thereabouts. If you can be sure of selling the car privately for more than the trade price, do so – anything above that price will be a bonus. If you do not sell the car, and have to phone up one of the dealers to take it off your hands, then you will have lost nothing, the trade price will be the same.

## Quick Tips

- The part-exchange price of your car will consist of two parts. A trade price, which is non-negotiable, and an over-allowance, which is the part of the dealer's profit that he is prepared to surrender to you.
- If the PX price offered differs considerably between garages, check the screen prices of comparable cars on each dealer's

forecourt – some may have been inflated to allow for higher trade-in prices.

Gain extra pounds by suggesting that the dealer writes back the VAT element.

Remember – the 'price to change', not the PX price offered, is all-important.

# 6  Initial Approach and How to Assess Vehicles

There are two ways to purchase cars, by the heart or by the head. If you are ruled by the heart – and we all are at some time – you will be more susceptible to getting a bum deal. Any used-car purchase should start with scanning advertisements for suitable vehicles and compiling a short list. This will consist, for each car, of brief details of its specification and equipment, plus a list of points to check and enquiries to make about it. Then – unless you actually like driving round for miles looking at similar cars trying to assess the pros and cons of each one – you will find it much more economical in time and money to make your initial checks and enquiries by telephone. In any case, at this early stage you should avoid personal contact with the seller. It is much easier to ask searching and possibly impertinent questions by telephone, and certainly much easier to say 'No thank you'.

To compile your short list, scan the adverts in local newspapers and the various free sheets and car-sales weeklies. For each possibly suitable car jot down the details given in the advertisement on a piece of paper (better than having to trawl through all the papers later, reading notes scribbled in the margins). When reading adverts you must learn to read between the lines, because the dealer has only a limited amount of space in which to list a car's selling points. Often it is what is *not* said that means the most. Low mileage, one owner, full service history (FSH), sun roof (S/R, or FFSR for factory-fitted sun roof), etc. are all selling points and will be included in the text. If they are not mentioned, then, invariably, they do not apply to that car. Check the other cars in the same advert to get a feel for the dealer's style.

You will notice that many adverts use terms such as 'usual Ghia refinements' or similar meaningless nonsense. This is because they have nothing positive to say about the car but need to fill the space (of course it will have the usual Ghia refinements – they were bolted on at the factory); cars advertised with this sort of description are usually ordinary at best. Also, the jargon used in adverts is confusing and riddled with abbreviations (used to save space, and hence money). RWW means rear wash/wipe, for instance, and T+T means taxed and tested. If you do not understand an abbreviation, and it is not in the glossary at the rear of this book, then phone for clarification.

Many adverts, especially for cheaper cars, may say 'slight attention required to. . .'. What this means is that the car is knackered. 'Slight attention' indicates a major problem that the vendor cannot sort out – why else would he be selling the car in this state? The fact that it is faulty will seriously reduce both its attractiveness to customers and its value, (if the fault is indeed slight, then surely it would make more sense to repair it). By the same token, any car advertised with no MOT, or with less than two months' ticket, is likely to need extensive work in order to get it through the test. A car worth around £1,000 or more will lose at least £200 of its value if there is no MOT, or only a short MOT.

## Initial Approach and How to Assess Vehicles

I have seen dealers advertise cars costing £2,000-3,000 stating 'MOT lost'. A duplicate certificate costs a couple of pounds if you go back to the testing station that issued the original, and a full MOT test only costs around £20. Why, then, does a dealer risk putting customers off or reduce a car's value by hundreds of pounds by saying the MOT certificate is lost? Because he knows the repairs will cost a fortune, that's why!

It is a good idea to use a set format, so that each car on your short list can be compared accurately. Head it with a short description of model, etc. then list all the relevant points to check – tyres, MOT, exhaust, and so on – and leave a column at the side for notes. Draw a line down the right-hand side and use this further column to make a note of any expenditure that can be seen to be required. Given ready access to a photocopier, anyone should be able to draw up a standard form and run off a few copies.

Once you have drawn up some sort of appraisal sheet, then you can phone the sellers and ask all your relevant questions, making notes as you go along. Before you even decide to look at a car, you need to know the following:

The exact make and model
The year of manufacture and registration prefix
The colour
The mileage
MOT and Road Fund expiry dates

If you are dealing with a private seller, you also need answers to the following questions:

How long have they owned the car?
Is the log book in their name?

Do they have a receipt for it?
Why are they selling it?

Any hesitance or reticence in their answers should be treated with suspicion. If you cannot get clear, definite answers, strike the car off your list. There are plenty of others to choose from.

If the vehicle is a limited- or special-edition specification, then clarify exactly what that entails. Many manufacturers bring out low-specification models as loss-leaders and advertise them heavily in order to bring people into the showrooms. Once they are there the salesmen try to persuade the customers into taking a more expensive model. Some special editions are no more than bog-standard cars with a sun roof and a fancy name, though others are better equipped. Ensure that you know exactly what is involved. The used-car guides list many of these manufacturer-created specials. They do not, however, list the ones that the dealer makes up himself (all it takes to make a special edition is a few stripes and logos from the local screen-printers and often that is all you will get).

One point to mention is that you should never bother to ask a seller about the general condition of the car. The condition is a matter of opinion, not fact, and usually a seller will give you a better picture than is warranted by reality, in order to get you to go and see it. Stick with asking questions that require factual answers.

For those lucky enough to be buying a brand-new car, much of the above is irrelevant. It does pay however to make some telephone calls in respect of any special deals or old-price models that may be in stock. A few pence spent on the phone could save hundreds of pounds. And, if you choose to buy from an auction you cannot make a phone call; the only information you will have to go on will be the details displayed on

## Initial Approach and How to Assess Vehicles

the windscreen – which may or may not be accurate or sufficient.

Once the short list has been whittled down you should have some idea of the merits and demerits of each of the vehicles. You can then rearrange it in your order of preference. The next step is actually to go out and have a good look at all the possibles in the metal.

It is not within the scope of this book to bring you up to City and Guilds standard in mechanical engineering. You cannot hope to diagnose accurately the faults apparent in every car you look at. Using an ordered, systematic approach, however, you can avoid the most common pitfalls and the confidence tricksters. When viewing a car, do it quietly and systematically, and without the seller or salesman hovering over your shoulder. Ask to be left alone if possible, or take a friend to decoy him away. If you have asked the right questions on the telephone, then there is no need for the salesman to be chattering away.

On a private sale, start by examining the documents. There is no point in getting all excited about a car that may be stolen, crashed and rebuilt, or generally neglected. The seller may actually be a small-time trader working on the side. The log book (V5), MOT certificate and service record all have a tale to tell, especially when viewed together. (If you are buying from a dealer, then you can leave this till last, but make sure that you *do* check them.) Once you are satisfied with the documents and the vehicle's authenticity do not put them aside. You will need to check the vehicle identification numbers against those listed in the documents. The VIN is stamped into the chassis and on a small plate that is riveted under the bonnet. The seller should know where they are.

Going on to examining the vehicle proper, start with the

bodywork. Stand four or five yards away and study the panels. Are they all the same colour? Then go to each corner in turn and look directly down the side of the car – any ripples or dents are more clearly evident from this angle. (To do justice to this type of inspection the light needs to be good; rain will render a visual examination virtually impossible.) The condition of the paintwork should be consistent on all areas of the car; any that are better or worse indicate an area of repairs. Run your fingers under the doors (they should feel smooth). Any rust will form here and on the wheel arches first, so check them too. Any car that has had bodywork repairs involving anything less than a top-notch respray will show the fact under sodium street lighting. It is amazing what this type of illumination shows up; if you are in any doubt about a car's bodywork, arrange to view it under orange street lamps. When you open the doors and bonnet make sure that the paint inside is the same colour as that outside. Peel back the rubbers to make sure. Any overspray on the rubbers, tyres or badges indicates that recent bodywork repairs have been carried out.

Tyres are expensive – and they come in fives, so check the spare. Make sure that the tread is sufficient. Any uneven wear may suggest that the tracking is out, the steering or suspension worn or that the car has been rebuilt incorrectly. (Do not be fooled if the wear is on rear tyres – they have probably been swapped from the front.) Hold the wheels firmly with both hands and try to rock them. There should be no play. If you can feel or hear a knock, then the parts are worn.

Whilst looking at the dashboard and interior trim check for unusual holes, sometimes masked by grommets, or extra wiring signifying that the vehicle has had a radio or meter fitted, and hence has been used as a police car, taxi or for private hire. If you suspect that this is the case then pay partic-

## Initial Approach and How to Assess Vehicles

ular attention to the roof, where extra aerials and roof-lights or signs would have been fitted; sometimes these are masked by the fitting of a cheap pop-up sun roof. Incidentally, ex-police cars may have been driven somewhat enthusiastically, but they will also have been impeccably maintained – especially the larger road traffic cars and those used for driving instruction. Taxis and private hire vehicles, on the other hand, are often run on a tight budget.

It is no good buying a car and then finding out you cannot get comfortable in it because of a faulty seat. Sit in the driver's seat and adjust it to your liking. While you are there, turn on the ignition and try the wipers, indicators and anything else that you fancy (they will all cost money if they are broken). Start the engine (with a diesel, ensure that it is absolutely cold before you do so – if it has been run recently then come back some other time). As you turn the key look in the mirror: blue smoke means a worn engine, whether petrol or diesel. Reluctance to start, particularly on diesels, can be expensive as can excessive rattling noises.

With the engine running push the brake pedal down. Anything more than 3 cm of travel indicates worn brakes, air in the system or leaking parts. With the foot-brake applied, work the hand-brake. It should only travel four or five notches – any more and new parts may be required.

With the hand brake fully applied and the engine on a fast tick-over, depress the clutch and move the gear-lever through all the positions (it is not unknown for five-speed gear-knobs to be fitted to four-speed cars). Balking, clunking or rattling all signify problems. Many four-wheel-drive cars have a second gear-lever operating the high and low ratios and selecting the 4WD option. Make sure that this is in working order. On automatic gearboxes the selector should be moved into all positions. The car must not creep when in gear with the engine idling and the hand brake off. Neither should the engine stall when the car is in gear.

Faulty power steering may also stall an idling engine as the steering wheel is turned to full lock; the front wheels should turn smoothly without juddering. If feasible, put the car into second gear and, with the hand-brake still applied and the engine revving at around 2,000 r.p.m., let the clutch out steadily. If the car stalls, all is well, but if the clutch or the hand-brake slips problems and expense are just around the corner.

With the engine running, open the bonnet and listen very carefully. Rattling or knocking sounds are expensive. If the engine bay has not been steam cleaned, look for signs of oil or coolant leaks; corroded brake-pipes are another indication of costly problems. Switch the engine off and examine the oil on the dipstick. If it is black, and the oil filter looks as if it has been on years, then the car has not been regularly serviced. Take off the oil-filler cap and look inside. White gunge indicates that the cylinder-head gasket may be leaking. The condition of the HT leads, battery terminals, hoses and brake fluid (brown is old, new is gold) all give an indication of whether the car has been looked after.

Look at the exhaust for any oily, black deposits inside the tailpipe (these indicate a worn engine). All exhausts will show signs of rusting within weeks of being fitted, and in any case they usually rust worse from within. Check instead for temporary exhaust repairs: welding or exhaust bandages.

Without having moved the car an inch, you should now have a pretty good idea of whether it is in good condition and what faults there are, if any.

Used-car dealers will usually stand the cars on their pitch

## Initial Approach and How to Assess Vehicles

just as they came in from the previous owner, cosmetic details aside. If you find any major (or indeed minor) problems, but decide to buy the car providing they are rectified, then make sure both that this stipulation is included in the contract and that the car is checked before payment to see that it has been met. Whilst at the pitch or showroom, have a good look round the other cars in stock. This will give you an idea of the type of trader or dealer you are looking to do business with. Are the cars well prepared and valeted? How many appear to have had major bodywork repairs? On a pitch of say twenty cars of around three to five years old you would expect three or four to show signs of repainting or bodywork repairs. If the majority appear to have been recently painted, then alarm bells should start to ring, and it would be wise to look elsewhere.

Many garages advertise one-owner company cars with full service history; these should have a service record completed by the franchise dealer. Such vehicles will usually have been well maintained. The tyres will be top brands, and engine consumables, such as hoses and oil-filters, will bear the manufacturer's name. If they do not, then the car is not what it is portrayed as and may be an accident rebuild or stolen/recovered. Always insist that the dealer confirms in writing that the car is clear on HPI, i.e. it has not been involved in an accident or theft claim and there is no outstanding hire-purchase levy on it.

Dealers who supply cars with full MOTs usually have an arrangement with a friendly testing station. It may be prudent, if feasible, to nominate a neutral garage (or one known to you) for the MOT test.

Sooner or later you will, or should, test-drive the car of your choice. If the drive is arranged through a large company you will find that everything has been arranged to present the car in its best light. The route is likely to be smooth, fast and traffic-free, and your salesman will drive first; his experience with different cars should ensure that the car will perform well. When it is your turn, make sure that the radio is off and ask the salesman to be quiet, so that you can hear any squeaks, rattles or other noises. You need to find a quiet stretch of road – though an industrial estate is best. Drive at around 30 m.p.h. and slowly take your hands off the steering wheel. Any tendency for the car to veer left or right may signify tyre, tracking or suspension wear; it may also be a sign of a rebuilt bent car. (Do not forget, though, that any camber on the road will also cause drift). Repeat the exercise, this time braking progressively; any sideways movement could be a sign of any of the problems just mentioned, or of worn suspension or faulty brakes. Accelerate hard up to third gear whilst checking the rear-view mirror. Then decelerate, again checking behind. Smoke is bad news. Use all the gears, accelerating and decelerating in each. Any clunks, whines, rattles or untoward noises mean trouble. Automatics should change smoothly without any noise or juddering. When in top gear try the kickdown whilst keeping an eye on the rear-view mirror; the car should drop a gear or two and accelerate away strongly, without leaving a cloud of smoke behind.

Take the car to a deserted car-park or somewhere similar. Employ full left lock and drive around in a circle. Repeat with right lock. Any clicking sounds indicate worn drive shafts (expensive) or, on rear-wheel-drive cars, a worn differential (equally expensive). Repeat the exercise in four-wheel drive, if applicable.

Do not be fobbed off by a seller who claims that the faults you have found are minor. If this is true, why have they not been fixed?

## Initial Approach and How to Assess Vehicles

That, in a nutshell, is how to assess a vehicle. It is not 100% fool-proof – no system is – but, by checking all the major points thoroughly and leaving your rose-tinted spectacles at home, you should be able to sort out a good car from a bad one. If you intend to spend a lot of money on a car (and most people do) and are unsure of your own ability to assess the vehicle, then you can obtain professional help. Motoring organisations, such as the RAC and AA, offer an inspection service. A qualified mechanic will thoroughly examine the car and then prepare a report which will itemise any faults found and offer an opinion on whether the car is genuinely as described by the seller. This type of service is also available from independent vehicle-examiners who advertise in car magazines and telephone directories (if you use an independent, make sure that he is registered with one of the trade associations and holds more than a GCSE in mechanical engineering). Obviously this type of professional examination costs money, and you cannot afford to have it done on every car under consideration. Use it only when you have settled on a particular car and the seller cannot or will not offer a written assurance of the history and that the car is HPI clear.

Remember that the onus is on you to provide insurance cover when taking a private seller's vehicle out for a spin. Do not be tempted to risk a drive without being covered. You will be driving a strange vehicle that will handle differently to your own, and all sorts of things will be on your mind. Don't chance it. If necessary, ask the owner to drive; you can direct him into carrying out the tests while you make notes.

### Quick Tips

Draw up a uniform check list for each vehicle being considered, to allow for easy comparisons.

Sort the wheat from the chaff on the phone.

Avoid anything that says 'slight attention required to....' or those with a short MOT, or none.

Check all documents against the car's VIN plates.

Assess the vehicle as described in this chapter.

Trust no one!

# 7 Stolen Vehicles and Accident Write-offs

Every day of every year thousands of cars, vans, lorries and motorcycles are stolen. Some are taken by 'joy-riders' and raced around the roads and fields before being stripped of anything valuable and dumped or fired. Many are stolen to order – expensive foreign cars are often shipped out of the country in containers, or resold under a new identity in the domestic market. The market for stolen cars is not just for flash sports jobs or expensive executive saloons but includes humble family cars – these can be resold more easily, because they attract less suspicion. Recently, however, the main trend has been to steal four-wheel-drive vehicles, which are in popular demand and offer huge profit margins.

Stolen cars come onto the market in many ways. Thieves may buy an accident write-off from a salvage company (thousands are advertised in the motor-trade publications and free ads), or simply buy or steal the vehicle identification number plate of a scrapped car. There are disreputable scrapyards where VIN plates and log books from scrapped cars are openly for sale. Alternatively, blank plates, which are easily available on the high street, may be stamped with the chassis number of a write-off; an identical car is then stolen and fitted with either the newly stamped plates or with those taken from the scrap car. The stolen car now assumes the identity of the write-off and, depending on the skills of the thieves, may be almost impossible to spot as such. You will notice that I said 'almost impossible'. There are always signs that the thieves cannot mask. Of course, not every stolen and ringed vehicle can be positively reunited with its original identity, but the signs can alert a potential buyer that all is not well and prompt further examination, or suggest that they walk away from the deal. If the police discover that a car has been tampered with in this way, they will issue it with a new VIN and re-register it on a 'Q'-prefixed number plate. No 'Q'-plate vehicles may be subsequently re-registered.

Another common ploy is to clone a vehicle. Thieves steal a medium-to-high-value car, replace the door locks and ignition barrel and fit registration plates from an identical car – usually from outside the local area, so that the chances of it being discovered are remote. They then fill in an application form, stating that they have just purchased the vehicle and the log book is lost, and store the car until a duplicate log book (V5) arrives from the Driver and Vehicle Licensing Agency (DVLA). The name given for the 'new owner' is fictitious, and the address is commonly flats or other shared accommodation where the residents will later deny all knowledge of having received the form. If the thieves have picked a 'twin' with a long expiry date on its Road Fund licence, then the stolen car will have been sold on long before DVLA smells a rat.

A favourite method of selling this type of car is to park it close to a car auction with a 'For Sale' poster in the window. The thief may even canvass potential buyers actually inside the auction, as they look at similar cars to his own. He has a plausible hard luck story and a log book – who would not believe him, especially as the car is so much cheaper than the others?

Another hazard is the rebuilt accident-write-off vehicle. After being heavily damaged, these are assessed by a skilled examiner and declared to be beyond economical repair (if rebuilt by a professional garage, the car would be worth less than the cost of the parts and labour involved). Back-street garages can, however, put these vehicles back on the road by using stolen or salvaged parts to repair them at much reduced cost. The levels of workmanship involved in the repair may also be much less than professional, so that the car may present a very real danger to subsequent users. Check the pages devoted to these accident write-offs in the car-trade magazines; many have small photos of the cars for sale. Those described as having medium damage are usually so badly smashed up as to be unrecognisable – so imagine what the heavily damaged ones are like.

Badly bent cars require a new chassis, or to have the original chassis straightened out on a jig. A jig is basically a frame that the chassis of a vehicle can be bolted onto; chains are fastened to various points of the wreck and are pulled to bring the chassis back into shape. This type of repair requires a great deal of skill and precision, and any bodged job may prove lethal to the car's future occupants and other road-users.

New cars damaged in transit or newly registered company cars that have been involved in accidents also turn up on the market. Do not assume that because a car is nearly new it will be OK; check it out thoroughly.

If you buy a stolen car, and it is subsequently seized by the police, you and the real owner or his insurance company have to battle it out in court for ownership. It takes months and is very expensive, especially where solicitors are involved. Any vehicle purchased from a reputable dealer should have an indemnity that protects the buyer if the vehicle turns out to have been stolen. But such an indemnity does not always mean that the purchase price is refunded immediately. Disputes often take years to settle and involve lengthy and costly court cases to establish proportionate liability, so it is better to ensure that the vehicle is genuine before clinching the deal.

Most ringers – stolen vehicles of which the true identities are masked – are sold privately at the roadside, on small bombsite car pitches or through car auctions. People cannot comprehend why thieves should take all the trouble to ring a car worth a few hundred pounds, and their level of suspicion drops in relation to the price. What you must remember is that a simple ringing job can be carried out in a couple of hours for a few pounds – which gives quite a healthy profit margin. Also, there are older ringers that were done years ago and have not yet been identified as such, or the 'twin' may have been scrapped and so will not come to the attention of the DVLA. A car stolen when it was new might have been through three or four innocent pairs of hands over a number of years before someone checks the VIN properly.

Apart from all the checks mentioned in the previous chapter there are several things you can do to identify and avoid buying stolen cars and accident write-offs. One thing to remember when viewing a car is that everything should be consistent. A high-mileage car will have corroborating signs of heavy use in the interior, bodywork and mechanical parts. If there are conflicting signs – say, a worn interior but immaculate bodywork, or vice versa – alarm bells should start to ring in your head. There may be a plausible explanation, but check it out thoroughly. Once again, assess the vehicle in a systematic order, starting with the paint and bodywork, then moving on to the interior and finally the engine compartment.

When a car leaves the factory its paintwork should be perfect. As soon as it is driven down the road it will encounter stone chips, abrasion from grit and fading from sunlight. The first time that it is washed or polished small scratches will be left in the paintwork. Look at any nearly new car and you will see faint scratches – if the car has been hand-washed or waxed they will be circular; machine washing leaves straight marks. These become progressively more obvious as the car ages. Perfect paintwork on any car indicates a recent respray and should prompt you to question why this has been necessary.

Initially, walk around the car noting the general appearance. Stand a few yards in front parallel with one side and look down the side. Repeat this for the other side. Then go to the rear and, again, check down both sides. Looking down the sides of the vehicle at this angle makes any ripples, dents or bodywork repairs easier to spot. Paintwork that shows alternate bands of matt and shiny finish suggests that bodywork repairs have been carried out (on a banger this is acceptable, on a newer car maybe not so). Look also for any shiny patches especially on the doors. These could have been caused by signs, as used in private hire vehicles – the sign protects the paintwork underneath giving it a different finish to the rest of the car. Study the paintwork intently. Look not just at the surface but through it. Sometimes you can see faint scratches caused by filler being rubbed down with too rough an abrasive: a common fault on bodge jobs. A good paint job involves a lot of time dismantling, masking, filling, rubbing down with progressively finer paper before applying numerous coats of stopper, undercoat and paint. All this takes time, and hence money, and so bodgers cut corners. This is evident in the workmanship if you are prepared to look for it.

Examine the window glass and rubber seals, the tyres and bumpers. Look for signs of overspray or masking tape, which will suggest that a cheap paint job has been carried out. Look in the boot and bonnet – does the paintwork match inside and out? Examine the rear wings carefully: these usually form part of the bodyshell and, unlike doors and front wings, cannot easily be replaced. Any signs of body repairs on rear wings may indicate that the whole side has been replaced or repaired.

Check the door locks for signs of forcing. Most cars have one key for everything (or certainly one for all the locks), so if a car needs a gaoler's key-ring, this may suggest that doors or locks have been fitted from scrap vehicles. Examine the number-plates to see if their condition matches that of the rest of the vehicle and that they have been properly fitted. Sometimes there is a dealer's name on the plates. Does this corroborate any other signs, like the tax-disc holder, service record, MOT certificate or address of any previous keepers?

Moving into the interior, examine closely the screws around the dashboard for signs that they have been removed. All screws fitted at the factory will be in perfect condition, but any that have subsequently been removed, for whatever reason, will have the paint missing on the head, and particularly in the cross. On an odometer that is not digital all the numbers should be in line, other than those that are about to change or have just done so. If the numbers are not in line and there are signs of the dashboard screws having been removed, the car will undoubtedly have been 'clocked' (i.e. its indicated mileage reduced).

Examine the seats. On high-mileage cars the driver's seat

may be torn or have sagged; similarly, the steering-wheel and gear-lever knob will have worn smooth. The clutch pedal is another give-away: if it is worn then you can guarantee the car has done a medium to high mileage. If you are in any doubt about how to detect these signs then take a trip around the sales pitches when they are closed and have a look through the cars' windows, or go to an auction and compare vehicles.

As suggested earlier, everything about the car should balance. If the seats are like new but the steering-wheel and clutch pedal are worn, treat the vehicle as suspect. By the same token, if the number plates show a Southampton dealer's name, the previous keeper is from Edinburgh and the car's last MOT was done in Norwich, then I should be highly suspicious.

Do not forget to examine the service manual if available. Compare it with any dealer stickers in the windows or the dealer's name on the number-plates and tax-disc holder. Somewhere inside the car will be a VIN (vehicle identification number) that you need to check. Sometimes this is stamped on a door pillar; on other cars (Fords and Vauxhalls, in particular) it can be found on the floor between the side of the driver's seat and the door sill; and many foreign cars have theirs stamped on a door pillar or suspension strut. (If in any doubt, check with your local police station for the location of the VIN.) Check the VIN closely. If it is stamped in the floor pan, move the carpets so as to check that it is not simply a plate taken from another vehicle and welded in place – and if there are any holes or filler where the VIN should be, walk away from the deal. The VIN should correspond with the chassis number on the vehicle log-book and on the MOT certificate. (If the seller has not got a log-book then, personally, I would not buy the car.)

Whilst checking the log-book in relation to the VIN, make a point of looking at the date that the vehicle last changed hands. If it is recent, it may suggest that the car is faulty and the seller wants to get shot of it, or it may be that he is a small-time trader dealing on the side. It could even be that the car is a ringer or clone. Why not phone the previous keeper before making up your mind?

Beware the three-owner car! Melodramatic perhaps, but quite justified. If a car has been used for private hire it is likely to have covered in excess of 30,000 miles per year and been poorly and infrequently maintained. Traders know this, and the private hire company's name in the log-book is enough to send any knowledgeable buyer looking elsewhere. To disguise this, when the car is ready for trading on the hire company frequently registers the car in the name of a private individual – the manager or a driver, for instance – as the second owner. Once the log book comes back from DVLA they re-register it in someone else's name. This effectively removes the first owner from the log-book. So, if a car is around three to four years old and has had one keeper for the bulk of its life, then two quick changes of ownership – beware.

Under the bonnet, there should be a small metal plate, approximately 7 cm by 4 cm, riveted into the bodywork; the position varies according to the make and model but it should be easily accessible. This plate will be stamped with the vehicle's VIN, and the number should match that inside the car and on the log-book. On new cars the plate will be bright and shiny; with age it oxidises to a grey colour, and white pitting is often evident. Examine its rivets closely. They should match the plate. If the rivets are brighter, then the plate has probably been taken from another vehicle and put on by a thief; they should not be scratched or misshapen, another reliable sign of

The VIN plate is warped and the rivets poorly fitted – a sure sign that the car is a ringer. Thieves have levered or chiselled this plate off a scrap vehicle (thus causing the plate to bend) and fitted it using a cheap pop rivet gun which has left sharp edges on the rivet head. The plate should be perfectly flat and the rivets smooth, and both should show similar signs of ageing. Here the rivets are newer than the plate. Also watch out for new-looking plates on older vehicles

Sometimes thieves make obvious mistakes when ringing vehicles. Look out for non-standard badges, trim and accessories. In this example the engraver has managed to make the typeface similar but obviously has problems with spelling. Badges and body trim can be obtained from any number of sources. Just because it says 'XR3' on the doors doesn't mean it didn't start out as a 1.4 diesel!

According to the odometer the Volvo had an annual mileage of less than 3,000 miles. However, the numbers are not aligned which suggests that the car has been 'clocked'. The mid-range numbers on an odometer should be perfectly aligned with only digits that are in the process of changing or recently changed, not lining up. In this example the 0, 2 and final 4 are aligned whilst the 3 is slightly high and the other two digits noticeably lower

Overspray as seen on window rubbers and glass means that a cheap respray has been carried out. If they have not taken the trouble to dismantle the parts or mask the surrounding area then it is highly probable that they have bodged other areas. In such cases the repair rarely lasts more than a few months before requiring more attention

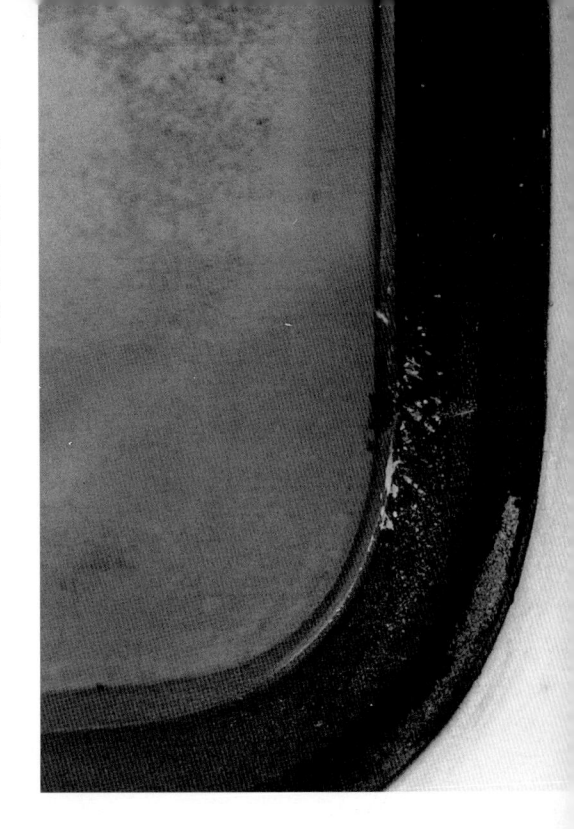

Uneven tyre wear could simply be due to the tracking requiring adjustment, or it may be the result of a badly repaired accident write-off. Cars that have suffered heavy accident damage may have been bent out of alignment. Rejigging requires expensive machinery and takes a lot of skill and time. If it is not done properly the wheels will not line up correctly causing uneven tyre wear and handling problems that often prove dangerous

This Calibra was stolen and stripped for parts. It will be auctioned off, repaired and back on up for sale in no time. An HPI check may be the only way of finding out its history. In many cases repairs are bodged and the car offered for sale on bombsite pitches or advertised privately. If you buy such a car in good faith then you will be paying over the odds. When you come to sell or trade it, and the potential purchaser spots the signs or checks HPI then, at best, you will be greatly out of pocket and may even not be able to sell it on. Should you have an accident in the car, your insurance company may refuse to pay out in certain circumstances a ringer's work, nor should the plate be bent or painted over. Bright, shiny plates on older cars may signify that a new blank plate has subsequently been fitted. Closely examine the actual VIN numbers that are stamped into the soft metal. Thieves can rarely match the flawless embossing of a factory robot, and any irregularities are a sign that all is not well.

Whilst looking under the bonnet check the engine-mounting bolts and those holding the exhaust manifold. Any signs that they have been disturbed recently suggests that the engine may have been changed. Look also for bodywork repairs, clumsy welding or areas covered in black mastic sealer – these are all signs that the vehicle has been in a heavy front-end shunt. It is also wise to check the boot for similar rear-end damage. Do not be afraid to pull the carpets and the trim back to enable a thorough inspection.

Engine numbers are notoriously difficult to find and read, so, unless the number is easily viewed, concentrate on the more obvious signs. For those who insist on looking, most numbers are stamped on the top of the engine block where it joins the cylinder-head.

By the time that you have got to this point you should have a good idea of whether the vehicle is as represented. If you have any major doubts, or a lot of minor ones, then I would suggest it is better to leave the car alone and move onto something else. Listen to your head, not your heart.

Do not be swayed by anything that the seller may tell you; even vicars will tell little white lies when trying to sell a car. If the seller is obviously shifty, take this into account. If he is perfectly plausible then remember that all the best con men are – they have to be. Do not believe anything that cannot be corroborated.

All stolen vehicles and those that have been written off by

insurance companies are recorded by the Driver Vehicle Licensing Authority at Swansea. A further record is kept by HPI (Hire Purchase and Insurance) who also keep a log of vehicles purchased under a finance agreement, with title to the vehicle held by the lender until it is fully paid for. If you buy such a vehicle and the borrower fails to maintain his payments, then the finance company will seize the car, leaving you to recover your money through the civil courts.

Members of the public can access HPI records for a moderate fee. Your bank or insurance agent can usually arrange this, or you can phone one of the numbers advertised in the motoring press; payment can be made by credit card. If there is any doubt about the authenticity of a vehicle, then an HPI check is well worth the money for peace of mind. Reputable companies will often advertise that HPI checks are carried out on all their used cars. If this is the case, then ensure that the invoice or contract is endorsed as such.

Motoring organisations such as the AA and RAC can supply engineers to examine a vehicle before purchase. If it has been involved in an accident or subject to a change of identity the expert engineer will spot it and report back.

If you inadvertently buy a stolen or written-off car and try to insure it, then one of two things will happen. Firstly, if your insurance company is on the ball, its computer will spot the registration number from the HPI list. The company will refuse to cover the car until it has been checked by a qualified engineer and, where necessary, rectified. Even if the company does not immediately realise the car has been previously written off, however, it will always check before settling any accident or theft claim. This would render your insurance void – no pay out.

If your current vehicle was bought from a stranger outside

an auction you will be forgiven for having a sickly feeling in your stomach. If the car is a clone, you will at some stage receive a visit from your local police officers – the timing depends on when the real car is due for taxing, or if it is sold on. Once DVLA realises that there are two cars, an investigation will be instigated. For people in this unfortunate position the only advice I can give is to make an appointment with the Stolen Vehicle Officer at the local police station and be guided by him. It is a criminal offence to dispose of any property that you know or believe to have been stolen.

## Quick Tips

Check the vehicle on HPI before buying.
Do not buy anything from outside or near to an auction.
Do not assume that nearly new or very old cars are OK. Check them out thoroughly as described in this chapter.
Avoid three-owner cars that have had two very recent changes of keeper.

# 8  The Salesmen

Salesmen come in many forms. The smartly attired, polite, attentive new-car vendors bear little resemblance to the scruffy, ignorant, sometimes less-than-honest people who deal in bangers. With precious few exceptions, however, they operate in fundamentally the same way – if you don't buy they don't earn. Salesmen are paid primarily by commission. They generate their commission from selling finance, warranties and accessories, as well as from the basic commission on vehicle sales. Generally speaking, the more profit they make for the company, the more commission they earn themselves.

Many dealers operate a system where stock losses are wholly or partially deducted from the monthly sales commission of the workforce. Stock losses occur when used vehicles are devalued by *Glass's Guide*. Every month the used cars on the forecourt are revalued according to the latest *Guide*, and the accumulated loss is carried by the sales team. They may also be penalised for charges on new cars that have lingered to the extent that they have had to be paid for. (When these old stock models are finally sold, the fortunate salesman alone is rewarded with a fat commission. That is why you may find yourself being steered towards a particular car).

In general there are two types of salesmen – the new starter in his first (and usually last) position and the old, hard-bitten career man. When companies advertise for sales representatives or executives they invariably state 'no experience required'. This is because this executive cannot execute. He is simply a servant, an intermediary between the customer and the Sales Manager, who holds the real power. You don't really need much acumen to sell a car. Most customers know basically what they want, having pored through brochures comparing differing makes and models, and invariably it is only the price that is left to sort out. This system of 'controlled selling' as it is known – which came, as you would expect, from the USA – makes for cheap labour. Salesmen come and go. They find the pressure of having to earn a crust primarily by commission too stressful, for the car showroom is a dog-eat-dog environment, in which colleagues think nothing of pinching a customer from their mate if they think a sale is imminent.

You can usually spot the old hands. They rarely wander about the showroom adjusting mirrors and arranging brochures but spend a lot of time on the phone drumming up trade, whilst keeping a beady eye on the forecourt. An experienced salesman can differentiate between lookers and buyers; it is a developed sixth sense. These people may have worked for the same company for donkey's years, or they may be journeymen, drifting from one dealer to the next and arranging their moves through contacts in the trade. When dealing with these experienced salesmen you will find that they know the parameters of any deal, and so do not feel the need to run back to the Sales Manager every two minutes. They will only use that option when you really squeeze them.

A professionally trained or experienced salesman is formidable in the close-combat environment of a showroom. His prime tactic is to gain your trust and find out from you exactly what you want; he will not attempt to sell you anything, or even steer you towards a deal, until he has finished his circuitous interrogation. Only when he knows exactly what you value in the product will he begin to make suggestions. You will do all the talking; he will use silence as a tool. People usually need to fill silence with noise, words, and he will use this to make you keep talking. Everyone loves a good listener – it makes them feel important – and he will be just that. This is not as strange as you might think: while you are babbling on you will let slip all sorts of things that he can assemble to create a buyer's profile. This helps him to plan his strategy, but it may also benefit you – salesmen know from previous experience that customers often either do not know what they really want, or are under some misapprehension about specifications or about the benefits of specific features.

A lady came into my showroom one day to purchase a small diesel hatchback. I could see from the part-exchange appraisal sheet that her annual mileage was around 6,000, so I asked her why she wanted a diesel. 'To save on fuel costs.' I did some calculations comparing fuel savings against the higher initial outlay and servicing costs of the diesel option and showed her that she would have to treble her annual mileage in order to make any overall saving. As a result she bought a petrol model.

This is why the salesman may ask why you have made your decision. It is in his interest to help you avoid mistakes and make the right purchase. By taking things slowly he avoids appearing too pushy, gains your confidence and puts you off guard. You may even trust him. (Comparatively few people that try to sell you a car are that good, though. The staff turnover at car showrooms means that you are unlikely to be able to go back now and see the same person who sold you your present car two years ago. Many are first-time car salesmen who will shortly move on when the promises fail to materialise.) A good salesman will persevere gently, shadowing your movements, constantly adding to his personal knowledge of your buying requirements. He will translate your innocuous queries into a purchasing profile. He will also ascertain your budget, method of payment, expected deal date, competing dealers and many other relevant points. You will give these vital secrets willingly in conversation.

The vast majority of salesmen employed by main dealers and used-car showrooms are paid primarily by commission. They have no time for tyre-kickers and families who roam the showrooms in order to pass a few hours at a weekend. Quite rightly so. While talking to a time-waster they could lose a buying customer to another dealer – or, worse, to a colleague. If you are one of those people who visit a showroom daily while trying to make up your mind, you will find it extremely difficult to attract the salesman's attention by the time you make your third visit; he will have marked you down as a time-waster.

The salesman who greets you in a showroom, shows you the cars and leads you through the deal – explaining prices, finance and valuing your part exchange – has no say in the actual price-fixing. This is all done in back rooms by Managers who take the salesman's assessment of your vehicle and work out a trade price for it. The salesman's job is primarily to extract from you the deal that you are hoping for. While you are drinking the ridiculously hot coffee (designed to keep you there longer), his Manager will work out the trade price of your part exchange and the profit margin in the car of your choice. He will then give your salesman an upper and lower

## The Salesmen

price for the deal. The salesman will then return to you and offer the lower price. If you have been silly enough to give him the idea that you would accept a figure lower than what they think that your vehicle is worth, then that is all you will be offered. The man's wages depend on the profit in the vehicle sold, and if he offered you the full whack in the first instance he would be losing money out of his own pocket.

Once you have exhausted the salesman's allowed margin and are still asking for a better deal, he will trot back to the Manager and try and convince him that you are ready to deal if he can find a little bit more to give. That is when the Manager sends some one else to view your car, to confirm his valuation before ringing round the traders for an underwriting (in the hope that one of them will offer more than he thinks it's worth), or else gets a more experienced salesman to put the pressure on you. If he is in a generous mood and can fiddle the figures to reduce his VAT bill, he may allow him to offer another £50. If you have managed to send the salesman back to his boss at least once and he will offer no more, then you have reached the best price the company will offer on that deal: the bottom line.

There is one common misconception associated with car salesmen in general. Customers believe them to be their enemies. They stand between them and their dream car and must be overcome, despite their superior negotiating skills and secret ways. The truth is that any salesman employed by a company and paid on commission is actually on your side. If you do not buy, he does not get paid. Rather than place obstacles in your path he will, if treated right, work with you against the big bad Sales Manager. It is the Manager who sets the boundaries; the salesman merely tries to maximise his commission. If you negotiate strongly whilst showing a commitment to actually buying a car, then he will do everything to make your purchase possible. Even if the deal is not that profitable he will still get a minimum commission. By working with the salesman, rather than against him, you have a better chance of reaching the bottom line.

Of course the owner-operator of a sales pitch will be a harder nut to crack. He has more than a vested interest in profits, and there is no one else to play him off against. He will still want you to deal, though. Any time spent with a customer is an investment, and he would rather have a return, no matter how small, than lose the chance of a deal.

At one time salesmen were always keen to offer test drives, as they often lead to a sale. It put you under a sort of obligation – once you had actually driven the car you felt obliged to buy it. Still popular is the 'puppy-dog' method – the salesman takes the car to your home, where it is seen by friends and neighbours who naturally assume that you have bought it (just try explaining to them why it has gone back, without losing face). Salesmen these days do not seem to offer 'on spec' test drives as easily; you almost have to be on the point of signing up before they grudgingly offer. If you imply that there are other cars and/or dealers in the equation, you will be asked to see them first and come back when you have done so. The salesman knows that only when you have completed your full assessment of the competitors will you be ready to deal – if he is last in the demonstration line, then he is first in the dealing situation. Forget about a test drive unless you can persuade the salesman that you are prepared to deal there and then; if he senses any lack of commitment, it will not be easy to arrange. (If you are fortunate, or convincing enough to wangle a test drive but subsequently let it be known that you need time to think about the deal or car, his disenchantment will be obvious.)

## The Salesmen

There are two things to remember when dealing with salesmen in any situation. First, never give any indication of the price you expect for your car, or have been offered elsewhere. (Indeed do not let them know that you have been anywhere else, as this smacks of a lack of commitment. Let them think that they are the only dealer in the world that you would trust.) Second, never give your phone number to a salesman. (Why should he want it anyway except to plague you for months at the most inconvenient times? Give him an invented number, another dealer's number or, better still, your mother-in-law's mobile phone number.) It is bad enough giving your address, but at least three years of invites to their wine-and-cheese parties can be binned without your actually having to explain why you did not buy from that dealer. The salesman will be offended if you do not give him your number – indeed he may try to trick it out of you with some ploy about ringing you when the new brochures arrive, or saying that his boss is away for the weekend, and when he returns a really special deal may be on the cards. The reasons for this are threefold. Firstly, if he submits a part-exchange appraisal sheet to his manager without your name, address and phone number, his boss will want to know why, and he will look stupid. Secondly, he will feel that withholding your number is a sign that you are shopping around, and are therefore not committed to dealing there and then. Finally, and most importantly, once you have left the showroom he has no further means of contacting you: that means that he is not in control and can only hope that you return. Do not offend the salesman by openly refusing details, though – after all, you need him on your side. Simply give a duff phone number. By the time that he realises you have done so, it will be too late.

The open-pitch salesman is a different animal. He usually

works out of a small Portakabin or caravan and sells older cars – i.e. over five years old. His approach is much more robust: if he doesn't fancy your part exchange, he will tell you outright or whine about losing money on the deal. One-man bands or small partnerships cannot write off depreciation against profits in other departments as major dealers can. If they have made a mistake and had to drop the price of a car in stock to attract customers, they invariably try to claw it back by reducing the over-allowance or discount. The major benefit of dealing with these people is that they actually do the deal – no running upstairs to the boss. Also, test drives are usually easier to arrange, but, once again, they are regarded as a sign of commitment.

When buying from private individuals treat the sellers as salesmen. They may seem genuine and really nice people, but remember that their sole purpose is to sell their car to you, not to somebody else. Lies will be uttered, truths withheld and all sorts of deceptions carried out during the innocent chit-chat surrounding your inspection of the car. Many so-called private sellers are actually traders making a few pounds on the side. They may be selling a car taken in part exchange that is really tasty and potentially profitable, or they could be supplementing their unemployment benefit by trading from home. Usually a quick check of the log book (V5) will show whether they have owned a car for long. Ignore any protestations that they had only just bought it when great-uncle Willy died and left them a better model; simply assess the car for yourself like any other. It may be a good deal, it may not.

## The Salesmen

**Quick Tips**

Remember, the salesman needs you more than you need him. Get him on your side by showing commitment and work together against the Sales Manager.
Avoid giving too much away in conversation.
Never let the salesman know that you have been elsewhere.
Treat private sellers as traders until you are sure they are not.

# 9 Special Offers and Finance Deals

'Guaranteed part exchange!' '0% finance!' 'Cash back!' 'Pay half now and the rest later!' How can you fail to get a good deal?

The biggest perpetrators of this sort of legalised deceit are used-car dealers specialising in cars up to four or five years old. Newspapers and magazines are full of high-impact advertisements showing how easy it is to buy a car. The ads often list several examples – some with 0% finance, others having a cash back part-exchange deal, and perhaps also a low-payments option – and are designed to include at least one type of deal that will appeal to you. If you are contemplating viewing a vehicle listed in such an advert, always telephone first. At best, the ads are usually several weeks out of date (they are created to get people onto the forecourt, not to sell any individual vehicle). At worst, they will never have had your dream car in stock, but will offer to get it for you if you leave a deposit – they will simply phone around other traders until they locate a suitable vehicle (which could in some cases take weeks), and meanwhile your deposit will deter you from dealing elsewhere (because, if you do, you are unlikely to get it refunded).

Let us look at some of the more popular offers.

## Finance Deals in General

Most companies would love to arrange your hire purchase, because they act as agents for finance companies and are paid a commission on their sales. The finance company offers the dealer a base rate of, say, 10% flat rate. The dealer then arranges your loan at 11% or higher. If, for instance, your loan is arranged at 11%, his commission is 1% (11%-10%) – £10 per £1,000 borrowed per year of the loan agreement; so a £5,000 loan over three years will net the dealer £150. If the loan is arranged at 12%, the dealer's commission will be £300. Your salesman will get part of that in his sales commission.

Frequently you also pay a 'document fee' to the dealer – typically £20 to £60, but sometimes as high as £100 – and this also adds to the dealer's profit. Ironically, most finance companies also pay the dealer a document fee for every customer signed up, on the basis that the finance house may get repeat business from them.

Go to a bank before you visit the dealer. Banks' rates of interest are almost always lower, and there is no document fee. Get the loan sorted out first, if for no other reason than that it prevents the salesman from blinding you with figures and clouding the issue when you need to keep a grip on things. You would not buy a car from a bank, so why borrow money from a car dealer?

Whether you borrow from a bank, building society or finance company, you will be pressured into taking out insurance to cover the payments if you are made redundant or fall ill and are off work. This is *not* obligatory. A lot of application forms have a tiny box surrounded by even smaller writing – if you fail to tick this box then the insurance will be added. Sometimes the sales person may apply pressure that borders on unethical

## Special Offers and Finance Deals

conduct by suggesting that the loan may not be approved if you do not agree to this option. The money market is cut-throat and, with normal profit margins squeezed, the finance companies need these insurance commissions to boost profits. Think long and hard before accepting this insurance, though; it is frequently overpriced. If the lender puts pressure on you to take it out, then say that you will go elsewhere. This usually brings a quick acceptance, without the insurance.

When shopping around for finance, remember that any outstanding loans that you have can be incorporated into the new loan. Many companies offer discounts for new business and will reduce the outstanding balance for an early settlement or an extension. It is often cheaper and more convenient to use your existing company.

### 'Minimum £1,000 Part Exchange Allowed'

Wherever you see this offer the dealer will have inflated the selling price of his cars to accommodate the attractive trade-in figure offered. There is not enough gross profit margin in used cars to allow for a minimum £1,000 part exchange; cars retailing at around £4,000 will have around £700 gross profit in them. The trader knows a deal like this will attract owners of old, cheap and generally knackered cars worth a couple of hundred pounds at most, and so he must put up the screen price to compensate. Check out the prices of similar cars at other companies; you will soon see the difference.

### 'Your Car as Full Deposit'

This means absolutely nothing. There has been no such thing as a minimum deposit since hire-purchase restrictions were lifted years ago. This offer is designed to attract the owners of old cars into taking out the dealer's in-house finance. The interest rate will be much higher than that on a bank loan, thus ensuring a fat commission for the dealer on top of his normal profit margin.

### 'Cash Back for your Old Car'

This involves the unwary taking out 100% finance on the new car at an inflated APR. Effectively the dealer is bribing you by offering to give you the cash value of your old vehicle in your hand, whilst charging the earth for the one he is selling you. Instead of taking out a loan for the price difference between your car and the new one (the 'price to change'), you borrow the full price of the new car, thus increasing the dealer's HP commission.

### Fifty-Fifty Deals

Sometimes these are referred to as 'deferred payment options'. Some new cars are offered on special finance schemes under which you initially pay for only half the price of the car, with the cost of the remaining half due in anything from one to four years' time, most typically three. The big attraction of this arrangement is that the monthly payments are much less than with straight finance, thus allowing you to buy a much more expensive car than you thought possible. This is because the payments are based on half the value of the new car, less your part exchange allowance. Assuming the new car costs £16,000 and you are allowed £5,000 for your old car, then the deal is worked out at £3,000.

At the end of the period, the customer can either pay the

outstanding 50% to own the car outright; or he can return the car to the dealer. The dealer expects the car to be returned in excellent condition. All scratches and dents will have to be repaired and paid for by the customer (at the dealer's premium body shop rates), and cigarette burns, torn seats, etc., will all involve payment of a penalty. The deals also stipulate a maximum allowed mileage. Exceed this, and you will be charged something like 6p per mile. A typical deal may stipulate 6,000 miles a year over 3 years. The average person's annual mileage is in excess of 10,000 miles, and if you are an average person the extra 12,000 miles will cost you £720.

The arrangement is like a time-bomb, exploding – often with disastrous results – at the deadline. At the end of the period you will not own even the half of the car you have paid for. You may keep the car only by paying off the full outstanding 50% (in our example, £8,000), and you will have nothing to offer in part exchange to offset the balance. Unless you have got this sort of money lying around, then a further loan will need to be arranged, effectively extending the car loan to four, five or even six years.

**Motobility Finance**

This is available to people in receipt of disability benefits only. Many of the drawbacks associated with 50-50 deals are reflected in this deal. When signing up for a car under this scheme be sure to read all the small print that deals with the allowed annual mileage and whose responsibility it is to have defects repaired. The scheme is not a charity, and many owners fall foul of penalty clauses that they were not made aware of when signing up. For example, if you burn a hole in a seat with a cigarette, then the hire company may insist that you have it recovered or pay for a new seat. Similarly, if your annual mileage is more than the allowance there may be a hefty payment due when you change cars.

## 0% Finance

This can come in two forms: manufacturer-sponsored offers which cost you nothing, or dealers' offers which cost you everything.

New cars advertised on 0% finance are usually subsidised by the manufacturers and advertised nationally. If you don't require finance, though, no price reduction will be offered instead.

Used-car dealers offering a 0% finance package are simply repackaging the deal to hide the costs. They may inflate the screen price of their vehicles or offer less in part exchange. They may insist that you take out an insurance policy through them to cover the payments if you are made redundant or fall ill, thus reaping themselves a commission from the finance company.

Salesmen will initially ask you how you intend to pay for the car. They need to know early in the negotiations whether you are intending to take out their finance, as this affects the part-exchange allowance. If you initially indicate that you do not require 0% finance and negotiate a deal to the bottom line, but then ask for the finance, you will find it is not available – they will have given you too much in over-allowance or discount to be able to offset the finance costs. (If such a thing happens to you, report the facts to your local Office of Fair Trading, as the dealer is obviously breaching the regulations in hiding the cost of finance.)

Watch out for special clauses in the offer; these may be

included in very small print, or even left out of the advert. Almost all the advertised 0% deals have an upper limit – say £5,000 on new cars and £3,000 or less on used-car sales. If your 'price to change' exceeds this figure, you will be charged full rate for the balance. Companies are obliged by law to provide written credit details on request. Ask for these details and then compare the total credit price with that from a bank or building society.

### 'A New Car For Only £20 a Week'

'Why £20? Let's make it a fiver. No, go on then, a quid!' Seriously, this is a joke. I could buy a brand new Rolls Royce for £1 a week. The snag is that I would have to find a 99% deposit on the £150,000 asking price.

Any weekly or monthly payment is linked to the outstanding balance of the deal: the price of the new car, less any deposit in the form of cash, part exchange or a combination of the two. It is also linked to the repayment period. If I could find a company that would lend me £150,000 over a hundred years, then I could still afford that Rolls Royce, even with a used Reliant Robin as full deposit.

When this deal is offered or advertised, study the deposit and repayment period.

### 'Cars at Trade Prices'

Rubbish! If a dealer sells cars at trade prices, then he is not making any money. He *buys* at trade prices and sells at *retail* for a profit.

What these dealers actually offer is third-rate cars – high-mileage vehicles in shoddy condition and poorly maintained –

that more reputable dealers would not touch. The trade price of a car reflects its condition; bottom book relates to an average car in average condition and with average mileage. But some cars are in such a state that they would not even retail at the bottom book price – hence the 'trade price' adverts.

You should consider why, if the cars are indeed at trade prices, the dealer is hanging around all day in his Portakabin waiting for customers? Why doesn't he load all his stock onto a transporter and sell the lot at auction?

### 'New Cars at Massive Discounts'

Are they actually new cars? Probably not. Large car-hire companies rarely keep their vehicles for more than twelve months, and sometimes for only six. These vehicles, along with manufacturers' representatives' cars, 'shop-soiled' vehicles, dealers' demonstrators and customer returns are regularly advertised as new cars.

Remember, a new car is one that has not been registered. Anything else is used – even if it has just six miles on the clock. Amongst all these ex-fleet cars there may be some manufacturer's rejects and damaged/repaired vehicles. Do not just take the salesman's word that it is an ex-hire car or whatever; check it out thoroughly.

### 'Full Cash Back in Five Years'

This offer originated in the furnishing showrooms. The company know from previous market research that only around 15% of customers actually manage to remember to claim the money back. Customers have a week or fortnight at most on the fifth anniversary of the sale in which to claim the full price refund. So many people simply forget to claim, or have lost their receipt, that the dealer does not need to hike his prices much to accommodate the claims – but he will raise them anyway. Most actually insure themselves against the cash-back claims, paying a premium for every car sold. Check out like-for-like screen prices to see how much the dealer has loaded his prices in order to finance the deal.

## 'Direct Cars'

I have lost count of the times that I have seen this advertised. Some companies even name their premises 'Direct Cars', and auction houses often advertise cars at 'direct from main dealers'. What does it mean? Absolutely nothing. A car is a car is a car, wherever it has been brought in from. It stands on its own merits and should be assessed accordingly. Main dealers do *not* send the cream of their crop to auctions, they keep it for themselves. They do not even check, let alone service, those going to the block. Forget any implications that this term may have.

## Swap Shops

A recent trend amongst larger used-car dealers is to hold 'swap shops', where they assess your car on arrival and give you a part-exchange price that is valid against any of their vehicles. Whereas usually the part-exchange price offered depends on the profit margin in the car you are considering (and how much of that the dealer is prepared to let you have), in these cases the dealers reduce the screen price of their cars to their trade price (i.e. what the vehicle cost them), plus a margin of profit. Effectively they are lowering both the retail price and PX price, and so in theory the 'price to change' is unchanged. From a customer's point of view, though, two things must be remembered. Firstly, they are removing any chance that you have of negotiating your own deal – they are effectively fixing the profit margin. Secondly, their PX allowance will be less than competing dealers', although, as they will no doubt make you aware, the 'price to change' is unaffected. By all means go along with their little game and compare their deals with those of others; you have nothing to lose. Indeed, if you do not like haggling then this system is ideal. But if you wish to (or like to) barter, do not be fooled by the straight, John Bull approach – they will still take a cut, if you insist.

## Free Gifts and Holidays

Many dealers advertise special offers such as free holidays or television sets. But remember, nothing is free.

Invariably the holidays offered consist of accommodation only; you have to arrange flights or transport yourself. Compared with a package deal, you could end up paying more for your free holiday than if you had booked it through a travel agent. Similarly, the 'country weekend breaks' offered frequently contain clauses that restrict you to eating in the establishment involved, at premium prices. Check out the quality of any electrical goods offered, and you will find them towards the bottom of their class. At best they will be end-of-range or discontinued models.

Ignore the offers. If the deal is a good one then do it, offer or no offer. Do not buy a car for the sake of the free gift alone. In any case, read the small print very closely. It is often not what the headlines imply.

## Special Offers and Finance Deals

If you find yourself wanting to buy a car that has a free gift offer attached, but you don't want the free gift, don't expect an equal monetary discount to be allowed. This is particularly true of holidays and weekend breaks. The company expect only around 10% of customers actually to take up the offers, and they calculate their costs accordingly. Therefore, if a dealer advertises a 'free' holiday worth £500, he will have increased his margin by £50 per deal to compensate. If you don't want the holiday, he won't offer anything like £500 as a discount.

Manufacturers' offers, however, are often worth having. Fitted sun roofs, air-conditioning and alloy wheels all add to the future resale value of your vehicle. Under manufacturers' offers these are nearly always added at no extra cost, the manufacturer subsidising the extra equipment as part of a sales drive.

Similarly, free insurance and 0% finance, when offered by manufacturers, does not usually add to the price. On the other hand, there would be no reduction in price if you did not want the extras.

### Quick Tips

Get a bank loan sorted out before looking at cars. Only take out the dealer's finance if it is cheaper than your bank.
When considering special offers, work out the true costs, look for hidden extras and read between the lines in the terms and conditions. This is especially important with 50-50 deals or 'deferred payment options'.
Avoid taking on 'cash back' deals, as they increase your loan.
Do not assume that advertised deals are cast in stone – the dealer will always negotiate.

*The Insider's Guide to Buying a Car*

Read the small print; look for hidden pitfalls and exclusions. Check out the quality of goods offered.

# 10 Warranties

If ever there was something that wasn't worth the paper it was written on it should be a warranty. Most warranties are so full of exclusion clauses and small print as to make them worthless. The salesman will tell you that the warranty covers all major mechanical and electrical components against breakdown. That is correct; what constitutes a major component, though, depends on the price of the warranty offered. In all cases they only cover breakages, not wear and tear. Even if the wear and tear contributed wholly to the breakdown, and the offending part was already badly worn when you took delivery, the warranty will not cover the full cost of repairs.

The actual warranty document is usually an insurance policy paid for by the dealer. Once you have taken delivery, the agreement (and more importantly any disputes) are between you and the insurance company. The dealership is not directly involved, as the warranty is underwritten by another company – the salesman will refer you to the underwriters thus keeping the dealer's good name unsullied. With the advent of extended manufacturer's warranties there are some newer used cars that have a balance of warranty to be transferred to the new owner. This type of cover is far superior to most used-car warranties offered by dealers. If a manufacturer's warranty is applicable to the used car that you are buying, then ensure that this is included in the wording of the contract and be aware of the servicing costs that will be incurred in keeping it valid.

Just as with used-car adverts, with warranties it is what is *not* said that counts – lying by omission is very hard to prove. When you are looking at the car you may notice a warranty poster or roof display board. In any case, the salesman will bring the warranty into the conversation. What he will not do, though, is elaborate on the terms, conditions and exceptions contained in the small print (unless, of course, he is trying to sell you an extended warranty that is longer than the standard one – in which case he will dismiss the standard one as being inadequate. He will, of course, receive a commission on the sale of the enhanced warranty). It is imperative that you ask to see a copy of the warranty document before you agree a price. The warranty may not be worth having, and you can negotiate a discount if you decide not to take it.

Do not worry about being left high and dry if a fault develops. The first month is covered by the dealer anyway, irrespective of the warranty period, and anything that goes wrong in this time or any faults that come to light will be covered by goodwill and/or the Sale of Goods Act. This Act stipulates that anything sold must be of merchantable quality and fit for its purpose. A motor vehicle therefore must be able to transport you and your family around safely and reliably. There are further laws covering the safety aspects of motor vehicles. For example, a dealer selling a car with a tyre below the legal tread limit would contravene these regulations, unless he endorsed the invoice: 'sold as scrap'. Basically, if a wheel falls off, then the Act obviously applies, but if the radio gives up the ghost, then you may be on your own.

## Warranties

The legislation only protects those who buy from dealers. There is no protection from private sellers, and that includes auctions (the auctioneers are merely acting as agents between the seller and the buyer).

Like all legislation, the Sale of Goods Act is bound up in red tape and procedures. If you have a problem that cannot be resolved directly with the seller, the matter can be dealt with in the civil courts or through the local Consumer Protection Department. It will, however, take a long time to resolve and may cost more in legal costs than the job entails. There are a few exceptions. Some dealers selling expensive vehicles and wishing to preserve their reputation offer comprehensive cover. But even these insist on you proving that you have had your vehicle serviced according to the manufacturer's instructions – which often entails costly main dealer bills.

As we have said, most main dealers and reputable used-car dealers will give an unconditional one-month warranty, underwritten by themselves (indeed, most warranty companies will not cover the first month). This allows for any complaint to be settled directly with the dealer. The reasons for the one-month warranty lies in the trade-in procedure. You would expect that when a dealer took a car in part exchange, or bought one from within the trade for resale, he would check it out thoroughly. Wrong! What usually happens is that the car gets a good valet and is put straight on the sales pitch. Of course, any bodywork requiring attention is tidied up first, but dealers will not lay out money on servicing a car that might spend months stood on the forecourt. Similarly, it is no good MOT testing a car in October if it does not sell until the following June; the customer will naturally want a full 'ticket'. So they do all that after it has been sold. If the MOT runs out in the meantime they simply stick trade plates on for any road demonstrations. Even when the car is sold most companies do little more than a short service (i.e. an oil change, and MOT). Any faults will not come to light until the new owner takes it home.

When it comes to trading in their vehicle, most people fail to mention any problems that are not immediately apparent to the assessing salesman (sometimes the fault is the reason they are trading the car in). This leaves a nasty surprise for the new owner, who then blames the garage for selling him a faulty car. Many dealers do ask customers to sign a statement saying that, as far as they are aware, their part exchange is free from any mechanical defect, but this is more of a deterrent than legal tool. It would be extremely difficult, if not impossible, to prove knowledge of a fault, unless the defect was obvious – and in that case the salesman should spot it in his appraisal. Engine management systems are notorious for intermittent and expensive-to-repair faults, and after suffering several breakdowns a driver may simply trade his car in and pass the problem onto the next man. Unfortunately, though, it is the poor old dealer who invariably takes the blame, even when he has no way of knowing or finding out that the vehicle is faulty.

The upshot of all this is that when you buy a used car from a dealer you cannot be sure that it is totally without fault or has been thoroughly and exhaustively checked over, unless the dealer specifically advertises this service (even then, it will not have been extensively road tested). It is vitally important to examine the vehicle carefully before signing to say that you have taken possession of it. There have been numerous instances where cars have been damaged whilst being prepared for delivery, and the fault has been left unrectified. If a customer finds a scratch or dent after he has left the premises, few dealers would accept responsibility for the damage.

Do not think, either, that new cars all come off the produc-

## Warranties

tion line perfect. I myself refused delivery of a brand-new car that was still on a transporter, having come directly from the manufacturers. It had overspray on the bumpers and tyres and was three shades of gold. Mechanics drop spanners, cleaners spill cigarette-ash, delivery drivers scrape bumpers. Accidents happen – make sure you don't sign for someone else's.

New-car warranties range from twelve months to three years depending on the make. They all stipulate that the vehicle must be serviced according to the manufacturer's schedule. This means having it serviced at a main dealer or new-car franchise. If you fail to have the car fully serviced according to the handbook, the remaining warranty will be invalid. Make sure both that you comply with the schedule and that the dealer stamps your service record.

Paintwork guarantees may depend on the car being routinely inspected and any minor damage being repaired at your cost. A manufacturer will not compensate you for rust damage if it was caused or aggravated by your leaving a chip or scratch untreated. If the car suffers a minor accident and the paintwork is damaged, you will either have to get the bodywork professionally repaired or lose the balance of the warranty.

When buying nearly new cars check that the manufacturer's warranty is still current and that it can be transferred. If the vehicle is an accident rebuild or stolen and recovered, the warranties may have expired.

### Quick Tips

Read the warranty conditions before buying. If it is not worth having, ask for a discount instead.

Beware of warranties stipulating the requirement for expensive servicing.

## 11  Doing the Deal

Everyone wants the best deal when they buy something. But, unlike televisions, videos, washing machines, cookers, settees, etc., cars must be haggled for. The price advertised often bears no resemblance to what the seller will accept – his bottom line. In this respect car-buying and house-buying are unusual in most people's lives, and it is common to feel uncomfortable when asking for a discount or better part-exchange allowance. There is something in the British mentality that assumes that asking someone to reduce the price is tantamount to admitting that you cannot afford it. People are embarrassed to do this – a fact the car trade exploits.

When you enter into negotiations with a salesman you are going into battle against a vastly more experienced opponent. Drawing on that experience, or even on formal training in sales psychology, salesmen can tell when someone is keen to deal or is messing them around. They can subtly interrogate you in the most civilised way so as to find your weakness and exploit it. Despite their seemingly insurmountable advantages, you can still beat them, providing that you understand the system. Your tactics will differ according to whether you are buying new, used from a large dealer, or used from a small trader or private seller. Buying at auctions is covered separately.

Never lose sight of the fact that the salesman needs you more than you need him. Customers do not grow on trees. Only so many come along in a week, and if they do not buy, then he does not eat. Get him on your side and you are halfway to getting the best deal.

## New Cars

When you set out to buy a new car, you should always remember that it is like buying a tin of beans. The identical product is available from a number of sources. If you are specific as to the model, colour and trim you want, and you are in a hurry, then you may have to phone around several main dealers to try and locate a suitable car that is in stock. This limits your options. If you are prepared to wait, though, any dealer can provide the car, and this allows you more scope in negotiations.

Straight cash deals involving no part exchange are usually harder to negotiate, as this type of transaction is the least profitable for the dealer. Whether you write to each company or phone for quotes, they may take umbrage and fail to respond. A simple one-car, no-part-exchange deal, especially if the customer is openly canvassing for the best price, will yield such minimal profits as to make it not worth their while. The manufacturer's list price contains the profit element of around 17%. In a typical family car that would have an 'on the road price' of £10,000, the MLP would be around £7,000 yielding a gross profit of £1,190. Out of this the dealer must pay all sorts of expenses including the rent or mortgage, wages and commissions, finance costs, power and water rates, etc. At best the dealer will be left with £900 – and that is before you ask for a discount. Many people would expect to get at least £800 off a £10,000 car, so the dealer would make very little on this sort of transaction. Some dealers will ask that you contact them last, so that they can beat the best quote. Obviously you cannot contact them all last, so you must play along and let them believe that they are fighting for your signature there and then.

By spending a little time making preparatory calculations you can seize the initiative from the salesman. Tell him what you want; if it is at all feasible, and you negotiate strongly whilst showing a commitment to deal, then you will win the day. He cannot afford to lose any serious customers. Tyre-kickers and dreamers he can do without, but people who are ready to deal are putting food on his table.

It is possible to calculate the gross profit margin in a new car – usually around 17% of the manufacturer's list price. So, if the car of your dreams has an MLP of £8,500 (before Car Tax and VAT are added), then the estimated gross profit will be £1,445. (If the salesman refuses to discuss profit margins, then contact the manufacturer or concessionaire direct; you will find the address on sales literature.) Remember, though, that sales costs, such as wages, rates, etc., will be deducted from the gross profit. Aim to leave the dealer with a maximum of a quarter of the margin and go for the rest.

In the example above, 75% of the £1,445 gross profit is £1,084, which leaves £361 for the dealer. Reduce the manufacturer's list price of £8,500 by £1,084, then add the Car Tax and delivery charges. This total is subject to VAT, so add that and the Road Fund licence, and the result will be the discounted delivery price of the new car: the price that you should be aiming for. Your actual saving in this example, at the current rates of delivery charge, Car Tax and VAT, would be £1,274.70 off the full list price.

If you think that the dealer will not settle for a mere £360 gross margin, after discount, you would be surprised at how little they will take when the chips are down. Every dealership has a sales target to meet; every salesman has his own personal quota to fill. They look to make every deal profitable, but if they get the chance to move some stock at even a minimal profit, then they will. Providing that they can get hold of stock easily, such deals are feasible. On the other hand, there are some dealers who are in the enviable position of having more customers than cars for sale. This is particularly true when exciting new models are launched or demand far outstrips supply. Such dealers are unlikely to discount much, if anything at all, but at least you can console yourself with the thought of the reduced depreciation on these models.

From time to time some manufacturers will run sales campaigns. During these promotions they may offer bonuses to the dealer which effectively inflate his gross profit margin. These campaigns are always heavily advertised, and dealers will be fighting each other for extra business; if a salesman seems over-eager to meet your suggested selling price, then one of these promotions may be under way. This is one of the few times when dealers will welcome a no-part-exchange deal. I have known brand new cars be sold for as little as £50 gross profit (a net loss, in fact) just to move another unit of stock. Shop around, play one dealer off against the other, and reap the benefit.

Part-exchange deals are more acceptable to the trade than no-PX deals, particularly in cases that involve the trading in of newer (i.e. one- to two-year-old) cars, and especially models that are good sellers. The dealer makes profit both on the new car and the PX. When a dealer sells a new car the net profit from that deal is accredited to that vehicle. If a part exchange

## Doing the Deal

was taken, the net profit is the gross profit less expenses and the over allowance given. Any profit derived from the PX vehicle is also accumulated against the original new car in what is known in the trade as a 'washout sheet'. Subsequent part-exchange vehicles may also add to that original net profit. The washout is completed only when a car from that line of sales is sold without taking a PX against it. Some washout sheets contain the profit from only one vehicle (where a new car was sold without a part exchange), others may include profits from three or more. From a dealer's point of view, he would rather keep taking part exchanges in order to prolong the profit line. But, from an accounting point of view, the dealer fully recovers his outlay on the new car only once the final no-PX deal has been completed. Until then he still has some of his money tied up in a used car.

The fact that you have to take your car in to be assessed and valued in person (no company will give a value over the phone) entails that you enter into a discourse with the salesman. Never, ever, give him the figure that you require in part exchange; you can only lose by giving him this information. Also, never indicate any other dealer's part-exchange price, or even that you have been to another dealer. Always show commitment to doing a deal there and then, if their figure is acceptable. Let them believe that they are the only company in the world that you would deal with – at the right price of course.

The salesman's first impressions when he assesses your vehicle may greatly influence the final outcome of the deal. Always present it clean, polished and tidy. Even if the car is potentially profitable, he could be deterred by filthy seats and carpets or grubby paintwork. It is often impossible to tell at a glance whether the car will clean up sufficiently to enable them to resell it, or whether it must be 'chopped out' to the auctions or through the trade buyers. This simple fact could deter the Sales Manager from taking a risk and allowing a couple of hundred pounds extra. In any case, the salesman will deduct the price of a good valet from your PX figure.

Depending on the company's policy, he may take the car for a quick spin to check that all is well. None that I have known do more than a quick under-bonnet check, so any temporary exhaust repair or other bodged job is likely to go unnoticed and therefore unpenalised. However, most dealers ask you to sign a form stating that the vehicle is, as far as you are aware, free from defects. Do not be surprised if the salesman finds and brings to your notice any faults on your car. Quite often problems develop so slowly that you unthinkingly correct the fault as you drive; it is only when another driver gets behind the wheel that the spongy brakes or off-centre tracking come to light. If he finds such a fault ask him to demonstrate the problem to you. Apart from ensuring that he is genuine, it may save your life.

As described in the chapter about salesmen, the figure offered for your vehicle will be set by a Sales Manager located somewhere else in the bowels of the building (he may even be at the end of a telephone line or at a computer VDU in another town or city). The salesman will only be authorised to allow you £X before, like Oliver Twist, he has to go back to the Sales Manager for more. His opening quote will be several hundred pounds less than the dealer's bottom line. It is up to you to sit tight, showing potential commitment to deal there and then, and ask for a better deal. Unless he has been back to the Sales Manager at least once, it is unlikely that you have reached the bottom line. Do not sign up until he will not give another penny. At that point ask for another £100 or so, stating categorically that you will sign the contract for that price. If he refuses to budge an inch, walk out. If he does not follow you across the car park to clinch the deal, sit in your car for a few minutes, as though thinking it over, before going back to sign up. You have reached the bottom line.

You may be sceptical about this suggestion, but let me assure you that it works; I have seen it from both sides. Now that I have left the trade and got a proper job, I have to buy my cars just like you, and my good lady's Honda was purchased in just this manner from a local dealer. We came to an impasse after the salesman had been back to his manager twice. I offered to sign the deal offered there and then, providing he put twelve months' road tax on the car; another trip to his boss resulted in a concession of six months' tax. We walked out. Before we had got back to our vehicle the salesman had caught us up and shook hands on the deal. (When I was selling cars at a franchised showroom I entered many such negotiations. The Sales Manager would give me a margin to work on, but would always say 'do not lose the deal' – especially when the car that the customer wanted was old stock, or we needed to move some units. When faced with someone who will definitely deal if you find him an extra £100 or so, the salesman will always stretch the allowance – after all, it's not his money, and he gets a commission even if the deal is not profitable.)

When a part-exchange deal is struck your car will have been valued using the current *Guide* price as a basis for the calculations. If the delivery date for your new car is more than a couple of weeks, then your part exchange may be devalued, according to the *Glass's Guide*. Confirm with the salesman that the part-exchange price he has quoted is firm, and if so for how long (there may be small print in the contract that will require you to find extra money on delivery day).

## The Insider's Guide to Buying a Car

How do you know what the salesman is really offering for your car? You could always ask him what his trade valuation is. It is no secret, and most will tell you, once they are aware that you know about trade prices and over-allowance. If he will not tell you then try this simple exercise: ask him how much he would sell you the new car for, if you decided to give the old one to your granny and do a no-PX deal. Assume that he has offered you £5,000 for your pride and joy against a newer model at £10,000 – and that, after a bit of haggling, he would knock £600 off the new-car price for no PX. He is actually valuing your motor at a trade price of £4,490. How is this so? By reducing the MLP he also reduces the amount of VAT payable on the car, which reduces the final sales price even further. So an apparent saving of £600 actually only costs the dealer £510 – hence the trade price valuation.

You can check whether the valuation is fair by consulting one of the car magazines that list used-car prices and doing some simple arithmetic. Remember, though, that the prices they quote are only a guide, and that other factors are taken into account, such as higher-than-average mileage, bodywork repairs required, obvious faults, etc. You must assess your car fairly, in the same way a salesman would.

What is also of interest and relevant, is the difference between trade and retail prices. Whether or not your own car is representative of the 'average car' on which the book price is based, this difference remains constant. This is because the actual trade price allowed on a car is adjusted to compensate for any work needed to bring it up to scratch. Say the difference between top and bottom book in your case is £800. Then your car, valued by the salesman at £4,490, would retail at around £5,290. Check out the prices of similar cars. If they are consistently priced higher than this, then you have not been offered enough. But do remember to compare like for like without bias, and to allow for any work needed to bring your car up to scratch, otherwise you are simply deluding yourself. These two exercises will indicate whether you are getting a good deal.

Assuming that you are happy with the deal offered, you may still be able to save some money by avoiding tax. In our example the dealer would knock £600 off the retail price of the new car for no PX. This would actually only cost him £510 out of his profits, because the figure attracting VAT would be reduced (£510 + VAT at 17.5% = £599.25). For every £100 the dealer knocks off the manufacturer's list price a further £17.50 is saved off the final bill (at the current rate of VAT). If you could persuade him to invoice the new car at the £510 discount on the manufacturer's list price (thus reducing the final sales price by almost £600) and then allow you only the basic trade price for your car, you will save that £99.25. This type of creative accounting is done all the time, mostly for the company's benefit. Many companies agree a 'price to change' and then fiddle (sorry, adjust) the invoice to save themselves paying VAT.

Dealers will be more likely to oblige you in this way if your car is to be traded out – i.e. it is one that they would not normally sell themselves. If your vehicle is to be retailed on their forecourt then they may be more reluctant, because the VAT that you saved will accrue against the subsequent deal when it is later sold. Used cars attract VAT on the difference between the buying price and the selling price. Retail price – (trade price + over allowance) = amount attracting VAT. If the dealer effectively reduces his retail price by the over allowance to save you paying VAT on this figure, then your PX will be brought in at trade price and so will, if subsequently retailed, have a higher margin that will involve a greater VAT bill on the second deal. He can cover this potential loss by doing any deal on your old car the same way, i.e. fiddling the figures to reduce the retail price by the over allowance element. Eventually one of the cars in the washout will have to be sold at auction or to a trade buyer otherwise the dealer would have to ultimately absorb that large VAT bill.

Do not forget also that any extra equipment or enhanced specification that you order carries a profit margin to the dealer. Whether it is a manufacturer's option or something fitted by another company, there is discount to be had. For every £1,000 worth of manufacturer's extras there will be something like £200 of discount available. And, the more they knock off, the less VAT you pay. If you do not ask, they will invoice at the full price.

## Used Cars

When buying used cars, it pays to remember that every car is unique, but it can still be compared with similar cars by using the trade's own methods. It is vital to shop around before actually viewing any car. Consult newspapers and trade magazines, draw up a list of similar cars, not only of the type you intend to buy, but also of those similar to your own car. Compare adverts. You will see which dealers are offering huge trade-in prices; check their screen prices against those of traders who do not offer these inflated PX deals – the difference will reflect the guaranteed PX price. If the prices are not advertised, phone up and ask. In comparing roughly like for like you will find that the dealers that offer a guaranteed PX deal will invariably be selling much dearer vehicles.

Once you have some idea of the price of the car of your

## Doing the Deal

choice, pick out some suitable ones and make a list on a sheet of paper. Phone the dealers and ask any pertinent questions that are not answered in their advertisement. (Using the phone is much more efficient in time and money, and it saves you speaking with salesmen face to face, which will only confuse the issue at this early stage.)

Before viewing any cars, you need to work out the trade price of those you are interested in. Look in the vehicle guides and compare the selling prices indicated with the screen price of the cars you have in mind. You will soon see which have been inflated to facilitate higher part-exchange allowances. Remember that, irrespective of the stated screen price, the trade price for each similar vehicle will be roughly the same. Also work out the estimated trade price of your own vehicle. Use the car guide figure as a starting point and amend it as you honestly assess your car, just as any salesman would.

Once all your questions have been answered, and your sums calculated, you can amend your list in priority order. Now you are ready to do business. Spruce up your part exchange, if you have one, and go to view the selected cars. Check out each car thoroughly, without the salesman hovering if possible. If you have already got the information you need, he need not be there while you examine the car, so ask him to leave you alone. If he will not do so, either ignore him totally or walk away – the last thing you want is to have him prattling on or interrogating you while you are trying to do a proper assessment of the vehicle. If you have not come alone, watch out for him passing the time of day with your companion; this is not innocent chit-chat but interrogation, giving him ammunition for later use – against you.

Only when you have finished your inspection and are happy with the vehicle should you enter into conversation with the salesman. If you have done your homework on the telephone there will be little to discuss about the car, unless you have spotted some point that needs clarifying. Ask him for the 'price to change': his car for yours. Ignore all the flannel that he will almost invariably come out with (most salesmen do not know when to shut up) and concentrate only on the deal offered. Having worked out the rough trade price of your own car from adverts and the car guide, you will be able to calculate what over-allowance he has offered. Compare this with your calculated gross profit margin in his car (the screen price, less your estimated trade price). Aim to leave him with about 25% of this margin and go for the rest. You should be happy only when he will not give a penny more – the bottom line.

When comparing deals from different companies do not ever forget that it is the 'price to change' that is important. This concept is the one most often misunderstood by the public, and so is exploited by the trade. If dealer A offers you £3,000 for your old car, then you would not settle for less from dealer B – yet the second dealer could be offering a better bargain, if the car he is offering is cheaper. I became aware of this shortsighted approach early in my sales career, when I had a customer who demanded a £250 part-exchange allowance for his rusty old Rover, which was a real dog – short test (less than three or four months of its MOT left) and full of holes. It was worth £15 scrap value, whereas the car he wanted retailed at £1,495, and I had only £350 profit in it. The most I would offer him was £200 but he was adamant: he wanted £250, or else no deal. Round the back of the garage, though, there was a vehicle nearly identical to the one he wanted to buy (a different colour but similar in age, condition and mileage). It had just been traded in and was waiting to be cleaned. I took him to

## Doing the Deal

this car and said that I could stretch to £250 if he took it as it was for £1,595. He accepted, without asking why these two nearly identical cars were priced differently. In actual fact they stood me at the same trade price, and the second car was to be retailed at exactly the same price as the first. My customer was blinkered into getting what to him was a good allowance for his old Rover, so he got it, but paid £50 over the odds for a car that needed cleaning. The mark of a good salesman is that his customer is happy at being taken for a ride.

The 'price to change' is all important – never forget that.

Where finance is concerned, my advice is always to sort it out first – at your own bank or building society. If you really must use the dealer's finance, then make sure that he is not loading the interest. If he knows you are paying the balance by his finance, you will have a devil of a job getting him to tell you the 'price to change'; the salesman or Finance Manager will only want to quote repayments. Ask the 'price to change'. Ask the APR. Ask about the document fee. Let them know that you are on the ball. Also, in law, any company offering credit is obliged to provide written details at a customer's request, and these details must include the total credit price. Ask for this. It will slow down the proceedings and give you time to study the figures. Do not let the dealer pressurise you into a deal that you do not understand.

When you buy from a dealer it is imperative that you observe the protocol for taking delivery. Firstly, do not expect to be able to pay the balance by cheque when you take the car. The company will need at least three days to clear the cheque before they let you have the car. Pay by cash or banker's draft and you can drive it away there and then. Secondly, if the car is to be taxed for you, make sure that your insurance certificate gets to them in good time. Without it they may have to tax it in their name – adding another owner to the log book. Finally, always check the car and documentation over thoroughly before paying or signing anything. If you take the car home and then discover a dented wing that you hadn't noticed because it was parked next to a wall, the damage will not be rectified at the dealer's expense. Accidents happen; make sure that you do not sign for anyone else's.

When I bought the girl-friend's Honda our agreement had included twelve months' Road Fund licence – they had offered six months, but I stuck to my guns for the full amount. On checking the car *before entering the showroom* I discovered that only six months' rent was on the windscreen. (Honest mistake, or trying it on? Who knows?) The point is that, once you have signed the document, any right of redress is greatly diminished. A dealer will not take back a car willingly, it costs too much. A friend of mine went to the traditional midnight of 1 August party to collect his new car; when he got home the sodium street lighting showed his nearside rear door to be a different colour to the rest of the car. At 9 a.m. he was banging on the showroom door demanding a replacement car, but, months and months later, he had to settle for a repainted door. (The car had been damaged at the factory and 'hospitalised' – i.e. repaired – and legally it should not have been retailed as new. These cars often get sold at a large discount or are run as company demonstrators). Because my friend had not noticed the repaint before he signed, the company would not accept total responsibility. As a Sales Manager I once refused to accept delivery of a brand-new car on a company transporter. It was three different colours and covered in overspray. Every day this type of thing happens to someone – just make sure it doesn't happen to you.

## Buying Privately

Private sellers invariably expect to reduce the price of their car from the advertised figure. Usually they have inflated the asking price to compensate for this 'discount'. Part exchanges are extremely rarely accepted: you are looking at straight cash-only deals. (If the seller has advertised for a part-exchange deal, or suggests that he may take one, then he is probably a trader. Check the log-book to see how long he has owned the car, if indeed he is even shown as an owner.)

For private sales take cash with you; many people will not accept cheques. If you do not have the full cash amount with you when negotiating, then you will not be in a strong enough position to get the best deal (a seller will often be tempted into accepting less than he wants if the buyer shows that he has the cash to pay immediately – a grand in the hand is worth the possibility of a better offer not materialising). Offer less than the seller wants, show him the money and come to some mutual arrangement as quickly as possible. Then take the car away immediately; if you leave it on a deposit and he gets another phone call, the car might not be there tomorrow. If the car is not taxed, tested or insured, then the best you can do is take the keys away after immobilising it with a steering-wheel lock or other security device. It is not a perfect solution, but better than being prosecuted for driving without documents.

## Quick Tips

Decide on the car and the means to pay before entering negotiations.
Spruce up your PX before visiting the showrooms.
Calculate your deal before entering negotiations. If you find

yourself confused about any point, ask for clarification (in writing if necessary), or take time out to consider your next move.

Show commitment and get the salesman working for you rather than against you. Remember, there are lots of other dealers and cars to look at, but this chap only has a limited number of customers to sell to.

Sign nothing until you have reached the bottom line – the lowest 'price to change'.

Before signing for delivery, check the car thoroughly.

## 12  Auctions – How They Operate

A car auction works like this. You take your old vehicle in, fill in a form and leave it. The auctioneers drive it into the ring on sale day, accept the best bid and subsequently pay you this amount, less commission. Simple. Or is it?

There are many pitfalls in both buying and in selling cars at auction. A lot can go wrong if you do not understand the written and unwritten rules. Primarily, the auctioneers want to be seen as independent agents. To a large extent they are: they work by taking commission from both the buyer and seller. They do, however, value their regular customers and ensure that they are looked after.

Most auctions have regular sale days, or evenings, when the run-of-the-mill cars are sold. Some cater for older cars, some for the newer and higher-value cars, whilst others run two or more rings to accommodate them all. Many also have periodical special sales – of goods vehicles, plant, accident-damaged cars and stolen-and-recovered vehicles. They may run a private entry (the auction house is booked by a company, but almost always open to the public) of collectors' cars or a bankrupt company's stock, including vehicles. These special sales are often only advertised in trade publications, so it pays to phone the auctioneers and ask what sales they have planned.

Auctions used to be regarded as the domain of the trader. This is now being challenged, as the benefits of selling to private buyers have become known. Dyed-in-the-wool traders resent the encroachment of the public, as prices, particularly of the more desirable cars, are pushed higher by its bids. In order to please both trade factions – buyers and sellers – many auction houses now run closed trade-only sales. Historically, traders could purchase all their used-car stocks 'at the block', as the highest bid usually reflected trade prices. Some could even make a modest living from buying locally unpopular cars at one auction, tidying them up and then selling them in a more suitable location.

A large proportion of cars entered are from new-car franchises and direct from large commercial companies. New-car dealers who specialise in fleet sales take a lot of part-exchange vehicles that are unsuitable for their used retail operation. The used-car manager at these dealers picks the cream for himself, sells the second-raters to other local dealers, and the rest go to the auction. Or it may be that the dealer is overstocked in one particular model, and any examples of this model taken in part exchange are traded out, even if they are in mint condition.

Fleet car operators, like the police, local authorities and large companies, also get rid of their old cars at the block. A hire-car company, like Avis or Eurodollar, may replace several hundred cars or more at one time, and the old ones go straight to an auction. It would be very difficult for any car dealer to value and deal with an influx of a hundred or so part exchanges located at various depots scattered all over the country, and the system also eliminates any underhand practices, such as traders slipping a company's transport manager a 'drink' in return for favourable treatment.

Sometimes, due to internal politics, a company may dispose of vehicles that are only a matter of weeks old. You would imagine that the losses would be formidable, but not so. When a major company tenders for fleet cars it does not have to haggle for a cut of 17% discount like you do; it would expect at least 30%. Manufacturers like Ford and Vauxhall sell most of their 'family' cars to companies and they vie for the largest slice of this market. It is good for business to sell to the company fleet market; the philosophy is that this puts the cars in the public eye, where they act as an advertising medium for the manufacturer. You will find that franchise dealers often offer super deals to clear one-owner, full-service-history vehicles of their own marque. Customers assume that they have been taken in PX against new cars, when in fact they are a job lot of hire cars bought at auction.

Whilst most private sellers actually drive their cars to the auction, company vehicles arrive in bulk by transporter. The cars are booked in, and all documentation is left with the auctioneers (if the seller cannot provide a log-book immediately, his sales proceeds will be withheld until the car is cleared). A windscreen sticker is filled out listing the make, model, registration number, year of registration, MOT and tax expiry dates, mileage and any warranty offered. The mileage displayed on the odometer may be incorrect; if it cannot be verified, then this fact will be made clear. There is also a box for free text that can be used to list salient selling points, such as one owner, good runner, direct from main dealer or direct from major company, etc. Some stickers also show whether a radio or spare wheel are included. Each sticker is endorsed with a lot number, which is important if you want to check up on any point at the office. (The lot number should also relate to the car's position in the selling order, though quite often lots are sold out of sequence.) The cars are then 'lotted up' in their respective blocks; you will find all the prestige cars parked together, for example. The auctions are open for viewing most days, whether there is a sale or not – although they will (or should) be locked, so any inspection is limited.

The seller may have stipulated a reserve price, below which the vehicle may not be sold. If the bids fall just short of the reserve then the auctioneer may sell it provisionally, subject to confirming with the seller whether he will accept the bid. But if the highest bid falls well short of the reserve, then the car will be taken away unsold. A car is only definitely sold when the auctioneer's hammer falls.

If he says 'sold provisionally', then the auctioneers will first seek advice before rectifying the sale. In either of these two cases the buyer or highest bidder is expected to go immediately to the rostrum and pay the required deposit in cash. (On a banger auction this may be £50; on newer cars the deposit could be £200, or even 10% of the sale price.) If a car is sold provisionally, the auctioneer's staff will try and contact the seller as soon as possible. However, they will be very busy, and it may take around half an hour or more (assuming the vendor can be contacted) before the provisional buyer can find out the position regarding his bid. When the staff contact the seller they will tell him the bid received, and it is up to him whether he accepts it. Sometimes he will ask the buyer to meet him halfway between the reserve and bid price (that is why you should examine the car thoroughly while you are waiting). You can either negotiate with the seller, via the auction staff, or ask for your deposit back. However, if the seller at any time accepts the bid that provisionally bought the car, or any concession that you have subsequently made, then you are obliged to buy it. They have your deposit, so there is no turning back.

## Auctions – How They Operate

Obviously the auctioneer will be an expert on used-car prices. He will know if a reserve is over-priced and will advise the seller on that point once the vehicle has been through the ring. He may suggest that the car will not fetch more, or, conversely, he may offer the opinion that on another day it might reach its reserve. The seller is charged commission every time the car goes through the sale, though, and so he may decide to cut his losses and accept your initial bid or the negotiated deal.

I have bought several cars in this way. Indeed my present car was bought provisionally and later finalised on the telephone. If the auction staff are negotiating with the seller by telephone while you are present then you can really have him over a barrel. I usually make a slight concession to my original bid and, if this is rejected, firmly ask for my deposit back. It always works; the seller cannot bear to think of possibly his only buyer being lost. He knows the car would be unlikely to fetch a better bid next time (it is always the fresh stock that attracts the most interest), and he knows that he faces further sales charges every time that it goes through the ring. When the auction staff tell him 'No, he's not interested. He wants his deposit' the seller instantaneously grabs at the offer. (If this ruse fails there is nothing to stop you going back later and offering more – if the car is worth it.)

If the auctioneer says 'not today', or something similar, and the car is driven away, then the bids have not reached the reserve or what is, in his opinion, a fair price. This sometimes happens when buyers are tired or jaded by uninspiring entries. Cars that have not sold are parked up and the sellers later informed, usually the next day. They may be re-entered or taken away.

While still on the premises, though, the cars are for sale.

Before a car goes through the ring for the first time the staff will not state the reserve price, or confirm that it has one. But once it has gone through and has not been sold, then they may tell you what the reserve is. This is used-car heaven: dozens, if not hundreds, of cars ranging from a few months old to twenty years or more, desperate for buyers at trade prices. There are no salesmen to confuse the issue, just you, the car and your used-car price guide.

All the same, it is very important not to get carried away and fail to assess properly every car that you are considering buying. The brother of a friend of mine, a man known for being tight-fisted (he owes nothing on his house, has over £100,000 in the bank and gets his clothes from bereavement stalls), bought a four-year-old Peugeot diesel estate from an auction after it had failed to meet its reserve in the ring. He thought that he had pinched it when his cheeky offer of £3,600 was accepted (bottom book was £4,600 and the reserve £4,200).

As soon as I saw the car I thought 'taxi'. There was a small, rather obvious sticker on the rear bumper that covered two small holes where the hackney plate had been fixed; rectangular shiny patches on the front doors contrasted with the dull, matt finish on the rest of the car; and the recorded mileage was just over 40,000, but the numbers were all over the place. If I had taken the time to examine it all thoroughly, I am sure that there would have been stray wires under the dashboard and three owners in the log book, two of them very recent. He sold the car a couple of months later for less than £3,500 after spending several hundred on the brakes and nearly £1,000 on a futile cylinder-head repair (it actually needed a new head) – greed had blinded his judgement. Just because the sticker says the car has never been used as a taxi, that doesn't mean it hasn't been one, and the seller will deny any knowledge and plead innocence. (In fact, if the matter had been brought to the auction staff's attention quickly enough, they would have frozen the seller's pay out until an agreement had been reached.)

The downside of assessing auction cars is that you cannot test drive them, though you may be able to get one of the staff to open a car up for you and maybe even start it. But do not expect this service during a sale, when the staff are busy.

Most reputable auctions offer an indemnity against the newer vehicles having been stolen or written off. They also cover the eventuality of a vehicle having been a private hire car or police car. The indemnity will be mentioned in their terms and conditions, should be clearly stated on the windscreen stickers, and will be referred to by the auctioneer. If the vehicle is suspected of contravening its advertised description, it must be brought to the attention of the auctioneers *within one hour* of the sale having been closed. They will negotiate with the seller on your behalf. You can either claim your money back or accept a negotiated discount.

The terms of the sale will contain a reference to any warranties offered. On bangers there are no warranties, unless the seller specifically includes one as a selling feature. On most new cars there are a range of warranties that may be offered – read these closely. These terms of sale are displayed in prominent places around the premises, and you should read them well before considering a bid. (I would advise anyone contemplating buying a car at auction to visit at least one sale as a dummy run before drawing their money out of the bank.) One point to mention is that the Sale of Goods Act does not apply to auctions.

The pace at which cars go through the hall is breathtaking to the newcomer; it is reckoned that a good auctioneer can average one sale per minute. The car on sale is driven into the hall and parked in front of the rostrum. The auctioneer states the lot number, followed by the make, model and year of the car. He will state whether it is 'on the letter' (i.e. bearing the later prefix for that year) and the expiry dates of the tax and test. The mileage will be declared, along with an indication of whether the seller claims it to be genuine. The auctioneer may also bring to your attention anything else he thinks relevant, such as that the vehicle comes direct from a main dealer or major company. He will do all this and still have time to sell the car within a minute, so it pays to listen carefully; he will not repeat himself.

The first four or five cars to go through often represent the best bargains of the day; the auctioneer wants to get the punters into a buying mood, and there is nothing like a bargain for causing interest. Amongst the entries will be some that have come from private sellers (they may need the money quickly or be trying out this method of vehicle disposal for themselves), and many of these have no reserve price. These cars will be used to stimulate a buying frenzy.

The first bid is usually requested by the auctioneer at a figure that he thinks is fair. Invariably the first bid is much less than half that, and initially the bids rise quickly. As the interested parties drop out the amount at which each bid is raised will be dropped, from £50 to £25, or even £10 on older cars (the bid margin is larger on newer vehicles). Before the first-time visitors and private buyers have comprehended that a perfectly good car is going for peanuts, the hammer comes down, and some lucky regular trade buyer reaps his loyalty bonus.

While you are still observing the sales impartially – that is, before you are intending to bid – study the participants. Look

## Auctions – How They Operate

at the chap towards the front of the seats. He came two hours before the start and studied every single vehicle. He has a notebook with the lot numbers that he is interested in written down; beside the lot number is a brief description and the maximum figure that he will bid to in order to buy it. He sits there impassively. In actual fact he is bored; this is his job, and the excitement wore off years ago. Occasionally he will bid with an unobtrusive wave or nod and if the bidding goes over his limit he will drop out. This man is either buying for his own used-car pitch, or else purchasing lots that go cheaply, so that he can trade them on for a small profit. If he is a regular he may have been rewarded with a 'quick knock' in the early entries.

There is another chap standing at the front of the seats virtually opposite the rostrum. He is looking for a nice family car. This chap will have no preconceived ideas about which make or model, so long as it will make a decent car at a good price. He will usually buy something with a little accident damage, tidy it up himself and then place an advert in the free sheets. Traders do not like buying work, and private buyers shy off anything that is damaged, so the car will be cheap.

There is another group of buyers that you will see at the side of the ring, where the cars enter. These young bucks swarm all over the car when something tasty goes through, spending the rest of the time in the queue of entries opening bonnets and peering into boots. They will have small car pitches selling top-of-the-range bread-and-butter cars like GTEs and Ghias. They clutch an expired *Glass's Guide* and constantly refer to prices.

A fourth kind of bidder is someone like yourself. He follows the car of his choice into the arena and bids with the enthusiasm that denotes a private buyer. Family or friends may be clustered around, all staring intently at the auctioneer. The private buyer is always in a quandary. Is he in danger of bidding too much? What about that other nice car going through later, it might be cheaper? The auctioneer will spot these bidders a mile off and may 'trot' the bidding up, especially if the seller is a long-standing trade client; the good price realised will do their business relationship no harm.

Trotting is carried out at many auctions though none would admit to it. Basically the auctioneer takes bids from a fictitious buyer in order to extort more money from the genuine bidder, who may be a private buyer or a small trader (they would never try this on a regular client). Once, by closely watching the auctioneer and where he was 'looking' when the alternate bid came in, I realised that I was bidding against myself. As soon as I twigged, I walked straight out of the hall leaving the car as 'provisionally sold' to the other bidder – not surprisingly, it went back through an hour or so later.

Despite what people may believe, a lot of cars that are sold at auction have nothing wrong with them. Obviously, the newer the car, the less risk involved. Providing you research both the prices and the individual cars first, and you do not exceed your self-imposed limit, then you will take no more of a gamble than in buying from a dealer.

### Buying at Auction

Buying a car at auction is unlike any other purchase that you are likely to make. The car will have to be assessed without a test drive. You know little if anything about its history. You do not know what price it will bring. And yet, here you are throwing money at it!

The gut-wrenching feeling when you are bidding is nothing to that felt when the hammer goes down. Instantaneously your mind fills with doubt. By the time you have walked across to pay your deposit you will want to cancel the whole thing. What if it is a ringer? What is the gearbox like? What have I done? If it is any consolation we have all felt these emotions; many traders still do have pangs of doubt the moment the hammer falls.

Except for nearly new cars there is unlikely to be any warranty or recourse if the car is faulty. The Sale of Goods Act does not apply, and 'caveat emptor' (let the buyer beware) is the rule at auction. Major mechanical faults, if not declared by the seller, may entitle the buyer to some refund, but the emphasis is on the word 'major' – if the wipers do not work, too bad. Similarly, if the vehicle has been declared as not having been used as a private hire vehicle or taxi and you find evidence to the contrary, there is a chance of a refund if you bring this to the auctioneer's attention immediately.

That said, there are some fabulous bargains to be had at the block. First you must choose the location of the sale carefully. It is no good turning up at the local banger auction if you want a two-year-old car. Check the used-car guides for the telephone numbers of the ones nearest to you and give them a ring. While you are checking what they usually sell and on what days, also ask about any special sales of vehicles that may appeal to you. These are frequently held on dates other than their usual sales.

Once you have settled on a particular auction house, leave your money at home and go and watch. Certainly take your notebook and used-car guide, but *definitely* not your money. Have a good look around the entries and assess a couple that appeal to you. Work out what you think that the car would sell for on a forecourt. Now reduce the figure to relate to a no-trade-in deal and make a note alongside the lot number. Check the terms and conditions of entry (take a copy, if one is available), and ensure that you note the commission charge and the amount of deposit required. Generally get a feel for the place.

As the cars go through the ring it will be impossible for you to check all the prices against your car guide, because the pace is frantic. Pick out the ones that are relevant as they come into view before entering the rostrum area, and look at the suggested prices in the guide, remembering to make a reduction allowing for a no part-exchange discount. Make a note of the cars that are sold provisionally or taken away unsold. Once the main business is over you can ask what the reserve was on those cars; they may even tell you by telephone the next day.

Only if you are sure that savings can be made compared with dealers' prices should you return with your money. Aim to arrive at least an hour before the sale time, to enable you to look around the entries properly. You should be carrying cash. No auction will let you drive away if you tender a cheque, and a banker's draft is no good, as you do not know how much to make it out for. Unless you intend leaving the car and collecting it later, take readies. It is a good idea to split the cash, keep your deposit handy, whilst making sure that the bulk is secure.

Check the cars thoroughly this time, as any mistakes will cost you. Assess them according to the system in Chapter 6 and work out the estimated retail price, less the no-part-exchange discount: this should be the very most that you will pay for that particular car. Make a note of the lot number, registration mark and your top price.

When the staff begin to assemble the entries for sale you should be able to work out the running order based on the lot numbers. They start in good time, so do not be rushed. If possible, be around the chosen cars when the staff start them up. Do not be frightened to open all the doors and even pull the bonnet and boot catches. Plenty do, the staff are used to it. As a car that interests you approaches the ring, take your place towards the front, in view of the auctioneer.

Remember, the first few cars that go through often represent the best bargains of the day. If you are intending to bid on one or more of these, make sure that you are in the arena, in front of the rostrum when they come in. In many cases these first cars are sold quickly to regular buyers, so you may be ignored. If you bid, then make it quick and obvious.

When it comes to bidding there are many different ways – some obvious, others subtle or lazy. The first time you bid is important; you must catch the eye of the auctioneer. After that any subsequent bidding may be more restrained. It will not pay to make yourself seem too keen. Do not get flustered if he ignores you whilst the bidding rises; in actual fact he is only taking bids from two parties. If one drops out then he will ask repeatedly for any other bids, and that is the signal for new bidders to catch his attention. Once he has acknowledged your bid then he will look at you for a sign at every raise by the other bidder.

The period between your successful bid and the hammer going down will probably be the most stressful ten seconds of your life. It will seem like ten years as the auctioneer asks for any more offers. He will signal a firm sale by banging the hammer and pointing at the successful bidder. Should he say 'Sold provisionally' and not drop the hammer then the bid has not reached the reserve price; there follows another agonising wait while staff consult the seller. If the auctioneer simply says 'not today' or 'not enough', then the bids have not reached anywhere near the reserve price. (Remember, though, these cars are still for sale via the office staff.)

If you are successful, then go directly to the rostrum or designated area where deposits are to be paid. They will ask all sorts of details from you – this is to prevent any one else taking your car, by mistake or otherwise. If the car is sold provisionally then it will take at least half an hour for the staff to process the transaction and contact the owner for further instructions. This is a good time to review your purchase and work out whether you will increase your offer if required.

Payment for the car will be taken at the office. The staff will ask you questions to establish your identity and ask for your deposit receipt, if one was given. You will then be handed any documents, such as the tax disc, MOT certificate and log-book; check these thoroughly before leaving. You will also be handed the vehicle keys and a receipt. Sometimes radios are kept separately from the cars, to avoid pilfering. Check the car over – in particular, look for the spare wheel if it was or should have been included.

If you intend to take your car home straight away, you must ensure that it is roadworthy and that the documentation (tax, insurance and MOT) are in order. Police officers get easy pickings from cars leaving auctions with the tell-tale glue marks on the windscreen where the notice was stuck. It is also sensible to check the oil, coolant and brake-fluid levels if practicable.

It is usually possible to leave the car for a day or so to enable you to sort out the documentation. (If you have paid by cheque, it would not be released until the cheque had cleared anyway), although, providing that the car and documents are in order, there is nothing to stop you taking it straight away. If a warranty or test drive guarantee is applicable, then the usual terms are that the faults, if any, must be notified to the staff within one hour of the sale finishing (this allows the auctioneers to check the vehicle themselves and act as intermediaries with the seller.) If you find such a major fault, report it within this time. Providing you are reasonable the staff will do everything they can to help sort the matter out. This usually entails a generous refund to cover the cost of repairs.

## Quick Tips

While auctions are independent, they may look after their regular trade customers.

Auction houses tend to specialise in certain types of vehicles. Some incorporate two or more 'rings' to accommodate new and older cars on the same premises.

The Sale of Goods Act does not apply, though there may be some means of redress if the vehicle has been misrepresented.

Once a vehicle has been through the ring at least once without selling, then the auction staff may tell you its reserve price. All such vehicles are 'on sale' and open to negotiation.

Match the auction to the type of vehicle required; there are many specialist sales.

Visit at least once to get the feel of the place and procedures before taking your money with you.

Read the notices on the wall and in the office.

Read the notices on the wall and in the office *again*.

Be decisive. Work out your top price for each car chosen, and do not exceed that figure.

Once you have paid for the car, check it out thoroughly and bring any major faults to the staff's attention immediately.

# 13 Selling Your Car Privately

If you are contemplating selling your car privately, it is important to realise the grief this can bring. I hate selling cars from home, although it sometimes pays off, especially if the trade is being mean about your part exchange. There are other reasons for selling privately – you may simply be getting rid of your car and not replacing it, or you may be hoping to buy a privately advertised car, or going to the auctions, where part-exchanges are impossible. But, whatever the reasons, think long and hard before embarking on this potentially stressful venture. Selling your own car from home is not always easy, and more often than not it can be a pain in the backside. If you are determined to try, then plan a strategy rather than rushing headlong into it.

First of all, you have to catch your monkey. The newspapers and car trade journals are stuffed full of adverts, so you have to work out how to make your car catch the buyer's eye.

Some cars are hard work to sell privately. Anything priced at over a couple of thousand is usually regarded as being too expensive for most private buyers. Anyone spending this sort of money is going to want an exceptionally good deal to offset the lack of warranty and dealer facilities. Also, the more expensive the car, the less chance there is of attracting a first-time buyer. The biggest problem with buying privately is getting rid of your old car. It is rather like buying a house – you can't buy until you have sold yours. And once you have sold yours then you need to buy another quickly to avoid not having a roof over your head, or being able to drive around, as the case may be. No one likes to be without wheels, even for a short time and so the promise of guaranteed part-exchange lures many people who would like to buy from a private seller. It is generally only the first-time buyer who is unused to having a car and so more capable of being without one.

There can be other factors too. Some models do not have a great reputation; they are slow sellers on dealers' forecourts, even with part-exchange deals, easy finance and a warranty. How could you hope to sell such a car? Try telephoning the sellers of cars like your own before placing your advert. If they are still for sale at the end of the week, then you will be struggling to get any enquiries for your own, unless it is substantially cheaper or better.

As for the advertising, forget about postcards in shop windows or flyers distributed at work. Quite apart from the complications that might arise if you sold a car to someone you knew, and it then broke down, the chances of such advertisements being successful are remote. You need to reach a lot of people. Look around you. There are thousands of different makes and models, each appealing to only a small proportion of the car-buying public; you need to sow a lot of seed, and much of which will fall on stony ground before you find the right buyer.

I would suggest that a weekly car-trade journal or free sheet may be the best place to start. At least their customers are actively looking to buy a car – whereas readers of local newspapers buy them for reasons which may have nothing at all to do with car-buying.

Your advert also needs to appear in the right category. Many journals have sections of advertisements for cars under £1,000, four-wheel-drives, prestige cars, etc. Your vehicle may fit into one or more of these categories; choose the most relevant one. For example, if I was selling a Saab 99 Turbo hatchback for £995, I could consider placing my advertisement under 'prestige', 'sports', 'hatchbacks and estates' or 'cars under £1,000'. I would choose the last, because that is the most relevant to this particular car.

Then the advert itself should grab readers' attention. Many feature monochrome photographs about 1 cm by 2 cm. What can this tiny image tell you about the car? Nothing! Forget about photos and go for a bold headline: '**SAAB TURBO, 87/'D' – £995**'. Follow this up with the car's selling points: 'long tax and test; 83,000 miles; full service history; immaculate interior; radio cassette and sliding sun roof'. Omitting a photo gives you enough room to avoid abbreviations and make the advert flow.

If the car has rough bodywork or high mileage, do not mention these in the ad. Obviously, you must answer honestly if buyers ask directly, but it is better to let them see for themselves because an individual's perception of condition is subjective – one man's Reliant is another man's Rolls-Royce. Avoid phrases like 'good condition for year' (this implies that the car has scars to prove its age), and terms such as 'good runner', 'used daily' and 'excellent starter' mean very little. Colour is important to most people, so it should be included. The interior trim is not so important, unless it was an expensive option when new, such as leather upholstery or Recaro seats.

Professionals can imply that a vehicle is a dream simply by including some features and omitting others. Customers want to believe that the car is perfect, so they gloss over what is not said, filling in the gaps with rose-tinted imagination. The best selling points on a used car either appeal to the buyer's dreams or reassure his wallet. Electric windows, alloy wheels and sun roofs all appeal to the former, while a long MOT and full service history will mean that he should not have to spend on repairs immediately. Similarly, no one wants to fork out on a Road Fund licence after buying a new car, so, if your car is ready for retaxing, get it done and raise the price accordingly.

Draft your advert on a piece of paper before phoning it through to the classified department of your chosen medium. (Don't forget that the journal will need a contact telephone number and your credit card details for payment.) If you know you will be out at work before 5 p.m. or later, include this in the text after giving your telephone number. Buyers will still phone before you get home from work on the off chance, but at least they will know to ring back later if there is no reply. (Answerphones are worthless in my experience – most buyers will not leave messages).

Providing your car is attractively priced and that price is not greatly higher than those in competing adverts, then you will receive phone calls. These calls may start around 7 a.m. on the morning of publication and finish any time after midnight. If this is the case, and the phone never stops ringing, you have obviously got a hot bargain on your hands (or you have underestimated the price).

Now, put yourself in a potential buyer's shoes. What goes through your mind when you are travelling to view a car? I'll bet you are already in the driving seat, radio playing, sun roof open, a fast empty road stretching in front; the car is perfect and it draws admiring looks from all, whether you are cruising down the high street or parking outside a country pub. Then you turn a corner and see it parked outside the seller's home – it is covered in bird-shit and one of the tyres is flat. Does this seem familiar?

When you sell your car you are selling someone else's dream. They want it. They want it so much that they have trawled through thousands of adverts, phoned dozens of sellers and driven halfway across the country to get to it before anyone else does. The least that you could do is make sure that it is clean and tidy! First impressions count. Nourish their dream, gain some momentum, and the little faults will diminish into insignificance. It is impossible to describe how important a good valet job is when selling cars – I don't mean just a quick jet wash, but a really thorough clean followed by a coat of wax (rusty stains visible in paintwork can be removed with T-Cut or something similar before polishing). Rusty or dirty wheels should be painted silver or hidden behind cheap wheel trims. The door-sills, boot and bonnet interiors are also usually forgotten during the weekly wash, yet when they are clean it makes a world of difference. Interiors also matter: scrub the carpets, seats and interior trim, including the dashboard and roof lining, with soapy water and a soft nail-brush. I then use a toothbrush to remove dirt from the vents and other crevices. Finish off with cockpit shine or furniture polish, and do not forget the windows (including the top edge, normally hidden by the rubbers). When you have finished, place an air-freshener in the car, or sprinkle a little 'Shake n' Vac' under the floor mats. Spending an hour or so preparing the car creates an excellent image that will impress any potential buyer; it also gives them less leverage for negotiating the price downwards.

If customers come to view a car, they are more than inter-

*The Insider's Guide to Buying a Car*

ested, despite any laid-back image they may try to present. Initially let them settle down; allow them to look around without interference. If or when they are ready to proceed, then go out with the keys and start it up. If they want a test drive, then ensure that the documents are in order. This means physically checking their licence and insurance (if you don't, you could be liable to prosecution if any offences come to light). State on the telephone that they need to bring these documents if they intend to drive – otherwise you must take them out for a quick spin yourself.

Most buyers open negotiations with the phrase 'How much will you take for it?' (what they actually mean is 'How little will you take?'). This is entirely up to you. If the phone has not stopped ringing all day, and people are queuing up to view the car, then I would be tempted to ask for the full amount – certainly from the first two or three customers. If this chap is the only interested party, then you may feel the need to negotiate. Put the ball back in his court, ask him for a bid – you don't want to knock off more than necessary.

If you can come to some agreement, then all that is left is to complete a receipt and hand over the documents and keys. You need to know the identity of the buyer, because it will take a few weeks before the car will be registered in his name, and during that time the Police National Computer record will still show you as the owner. (If the buyer commits an offence during this period, it may be you who gets a knock on the door or a summons through the letterbox, so you need to be able to redirect these attentions.) Endorse the receipt with the time and date. Also include the phrase 'sold as seen', so as to avoid any misunderstanding about a guarantee or warranty. Ask the buyer to sign the receipt. Complete the tear'off part of the V5 with the buyer's name and address and keep this yourself; you need to post this off to the DVLA.

Very few people have the moral fibre to say 'No thanks' or 'Sorry, it's more than I would pay'. Most will leave saying 'I'll think about it' or claim to be looking at another car before deciding. If they were honest, then they would tell you that the car is not what they visualised in their dream, or that they cannot afford it. Some people do view cars that they cannot afford in the hope that, by some miracle, the price will be lowered to their budget – 'dreamers', 'tyre-kickers' and 'time-wasters' are phrases used to describe such people. Unfortunately you will not be able to recognise them until the selling price is discussed. (You could ask them if they have the money before the test drive, but this smacks of rudeness.)

If your car is still unsold after around five days after publication, then you need to rethink your strategy. If you have had the presence of mind to obtain the names and phone numbers of interested parties who balked at the asking price, a phone call would establish whether they are interested at a reduced figure. Alternatively, another advert could be placed, with a lower asking price.

Private sellers of used cars are prey to criminals. Popular scams are paying with forged money, or coming back later to steal the car. Some crooks actually view a car solely with the intention of finding out whether it has an alarm or other security device fitted. Those that are vulnerable may vanish overnight. Keep a record of viewers' vehicle registration numbers and look around their car to see if the ignition is damaged (they may have stolen that one too). Never let them take the car out without you present (and do not let the potential buyer take a friend along for the test drive, unless you take someone too). Treat everyone as suspect until you know otherwise.

## Quick Tips

Choose your advertising medium carefully.
Phone previous advertisers of similar cars to your own, to see if they have sold. You might be wasting your time.
Spend time and effort preparing the car for viewing.
Trust nobody.

# Glossary of Terms and Abbreviations

| | |
|---|---|
| 4WD | four-wheel drive |
| 4WS | four-wheel steering |
| | |
| ABS | automatic braking system (anti-skid device) |
| ally's | alloy wheels |
| ATC | automatic traction control (prevents wheel-spin) |
| auto | automatic transmission |
| AWD | all-wheel drive |
| | |
| BHP | brake horsepower |
| block | auction |
| Bottom Book | trade price of a vehicle |
| | |
| cam | camshaft |
| carb | carburettor |
| cat | exhaust catalyser |
| c/l | central locking |
| clocking | reducing odometer reading |
| clone | stolen vehicle bearing another identical vehicle's identification plates |
| cyl | cylinder |

| | |
|---|---|
| DHC | drop-head coupe (soft-top sports car) |
| dog | car in rough condition |
| DOHC | double overhead camshaft |
| | |
| EFI | electronic fuel injection |
| EM | electric mirrors |
| ESR | electric sun roof |
| EW | electric windows |
| | |
| FFSR | factory fitted sun roof |
| FHC | fixed head coupe (hard-top sportscar) |
| FSH | full service history |
| FTT | full tax and test |
| FWD | front-wheel drive (sometimes four-wheel drive) |
| | |
| Hi-Lo | twin-ratio gearbox, usually on 4WD |
| HPI | agency that records vehicles that have been subject to a major insurance claim, have been reported as stolen or have outstanding finance payments due |
| HRS | heated rear screen |
| HS | heated seats |
| H/T | hard top |
| HWW | headlamp wash/wipe |
| | |
| i | injection |
| | |
| K | thousands of miles (e.g. 34K) |
| | |
| LS | lowered suspension |
| LWB | long wheelbase |

## Glossary

| | |
|---|---|
| mint | excellent condition (seller's opinion) |
| MLP | manufacturer's list price |
| MPG | miles per gallon |
| | |
| nail | vehicle in poor condition |
| N/S | nearside (left-hand side in UK) |
| | |
| OHC | overhead camshaft |
| ONO | or near offer/or nearest offer |
| on the letter | having the later prefix for that year |
| OHV | overhead valve (older type of engine) |
| O/S | offside (right-hand side in UK) |
| over allowance | difference between trade price and part-exchange price |
| OVNO | or very near offer |
| | |
| PAS | power-assisted steering |
| PDI | pre-delivery inspection |
| Pet | petrol |
| PX | part-exchange |
| | |
| Q plate | a kit car or vehicle of unestablished identity (i.e. a possible ringer recovered by the police and later re-registered) |
| | |
| rent | vehicle excise licence |
| ringer | stolen vehicle on false plates |
| RSB | rear seat belts |
| RWD | rear-wheel drive |
| RWW | rear wash/wipe |
| | |
| shed | vehicle in poor condition |
| SOHC | single overhead camshaft |

| | |
|---|---|
| SR | sun roof |
| | |
| T + T | taxed and tested |
| TD, TDI | turbo diesel/turbo diesel injection |
| Top Book | retail price of a vehicle |
| trotting | running up the bidding at auction |
| twin cam | twin camshaft |
| | |
| V5 | vehicle registration document (log book) |
| VCO | very close offer |
| VGC | very good condition (seller's opinion) |
| VIN | vehicle identification number |
| | |
| washout | cumulative profit on a new car, the part exchange vehicle taken against it, the one taken against that, and so on |

## Buying a Bargain Car at Auction

### *Rupert Stock*

To the majority of private individuals buying a vehicle, the car auction is a mysterious event attended only by car dealers who obtain most of their vehicles from this source. Moreover, from the fleeting glimpses of it seen on television, or in the press, the whole setting seems awesome and accordingly best avoided despite the tempting reports of some of the bargains obtained.

This book has been written, therefore, to explain all the mysteries, to remove the fears and to show how the private buyer can compete on equal terms with the professionals. Every step of the process of buying at auction is described in detail so that, armed with the invaluable information gained from his book, the buyer can make his purchase confident in the knowledge that he or she has bought the car at a competitive price with the minimum of risk.

Why pay 'retail' prices when you too can pay 'trade'?

*Contents include:*

Reasons for Buying a Car at Auction • Auction Procedure • The Sale Trials • Deposits and Payment Procedures • Arranging Finance for Auction Purchases • Choosing an Auction House • Indemnity • Choosing Your Car and Making a Move • A Valuation • Final Inspection of Bodywork and Mechanics Prior to Sale Bidding on a 'Not Sold' Car After Sale • Buying Nearly New Cars at Auction • Checking Your Purchase • Step-by-Step Guide to Buying • 8 Appendices of Useful Information

*216 x 138mm 128pp p/b 2 line illus. 0 7090 5628 1*

# Road Accident Compensation

## *Terence Baldwin*

Traffic on our roads is increasing, and so is the prospect of being involved in an accident. More than a million people each year have a right to compensation for injury, car damage and many other losses, caused by a road accident.

Whether you already have a claim pending or you want to be ready should the need arise, this book is for you. It is the essential guide to understanding, and making the most of, a road accident claim. The author is an experienced solicitor who has written this book for you, the accident victim, rather than for other lawyers. He explains, clearly and concisely, what must be done to prove your claim, how to fund it, and what happens if you have to go to court. He suggests possible answers to those all-important questions: 'What can I claim for?'; 'How much will I get?'; 'How long will it take?'. Other topics discussed include claims on behalf of children and the elderly, fatal accidents, accidents abroad, and what to do if things seem to be going wrong. The book will also be of considerable value to those who find themselves defending a claim.

By knowing what to do in case of an accident, what you can claim for and what you need to do to prove your losses, you can be in control of your claim. This book is likely to pay for itself many times over, by helping you to give clear and adequate instructions to your solicitor. This will improve the chances of being successful with your claim, and of receiving the best compensation obtainable in the circumstances.

*216 x 138mm   160pp   p/b   0 7090 5811 X*